LA COURTINE: A SURGEON'S MEMOIR

1ST LT. WILLIAM C. KINTNER, SR.

LA COURTINE: A SURGEON'S MEMOIR

JIM KINTNER

Rights Reserved

Copyright@2018 by James P Kintner, JD, LL.M., All Rights Reserved. No part of this book may be used or reproduced in any manner whatsoever without prior written consent of the author.

All Rights Reserved as to the family photographs which are the sole and separate property of the Kintner Family. All other photos are non-licensed photos in the public domain.

ISBN: 9780692172506

PROLOGUE

This memoir is dedicated to the memory of Dr. William C. Kintner, Sr., whose service as an officer in the 164th Ambulance Company, 41st (Rainbow) Division, Fifth Army, American Expeditionary Force (AEF) from August 31st, 1917 to February 26th, 1919 saved hundreds of lives, under difficult conditions, often working near the front line. This story is based upon true events. The substance, places, and people mentioned in this memoir are factual, some details have been fictionized to enhance the story. This narrative was completed in time to celebrate the 100th Anniversary of his service. As his grandson, it has been one of my lifetime goals to tell his story. It is indeed a historic and honorable one. I hope you enjoy it.

James P. Kintner
September, 2018

CHAPTER ONE

War News

On Tuesday, the 27th of May, 1917, the day started just as any other day in my life as a physician. My name is Dr. William C. Kintner, Sr. and this is the story of my war service in the U.S. Army from 1917 to 1919. I was up early that day at 6:00 am to tend to my two month old son, Will, eat breakfast, make rounds at the hospital, and then go to my office for appointments in downtown Seattle. Little did I know that with the daily mail, my draft notice from the Washington National Guard would arrive, requiring me to report for duty to in the Washington State National Guard. I had moved to the State of Washington from my home in Indiana in 1909 to practice medicine. My love for the outdoors, fishing, hunting and exploring the wilderness had brought me to the Pacific Northwest. I had worked at a Crown Lumber as an in house physician tending to logging mill injuries for five years. I had started a small medical

Will, Jr. and I 1916

practice on the side, and had built it up with new patients. Now, eight years after my arrival in the Pacific Northwest, I was a successful physician with a wife and child. I was now being drawn into the military to serve our country in the Great War in France. The draft notice was like a thunderbolt followed by lightning strike that changed my life, in the time it took to open the letter from the Washington State National Guard. I was dumbstruck, and unable to verbalize words of any kind. My wife, Anna, asked me what was wrong. I just replied, I going to war per the draft notice. She broke down in tears knowing that she would give birth to our second child alone, without me. There was a strange sadness that filled the room. I told her that I would return from the war, and never leave her. These words would haunt me later in life.

I had anxiety about the war, the separation from my wife and child, and loss of my medical practice, and the possibility of the loss my life. I reported for my induction physical at Camp Murray, Washington on June 26th, 1917, and was commissioned a first lieutenant in the Medical Corps of the Washington National Guard. I was given my uniforms, side arm, a duty assignment and told to wait for orders to report for duty.

The United States had declared war against Germany in April, 1917, but at that time the United States had a very small standing army. The Selective Service Act was enacted May 18, 1917, authorizing the U.S. Congress to raise a standing army. The Act called for the compulsory enlistment of men into the military service. The new draft law was

Draft Registration Notice 1917

envisioned in December 1916, and brought to the President attention shortly after the break in relations with Germany in February, 1917. I was aware of potential of being called into service, but I thought because of my age and new family I would be exempt. All of my worries became a reality, as I awaited orders to report to the Washington National Guard. I continued to work and treat patients, hoping that President, Woodrow Wilson, would keep us out of the conflict. The bad news came on July 15th, 1917, when President Wilson called our armed forces to duty in the Great War. I was totally devastated, and depressed thinking, at age thirty two, my life could end in a war that no one wanted. I had spent hours consoling my wife, Martha, who was pregnant with our second child that everything would be all right. With her family in Kentucky, I had made accommodation for my wife and son to return to her family home near Louisville, for the duration of my service. I received news that I was to report for duty on August 31st, 1917.

The prospects of reporting for duty and being inducted into the military brought on the thought that I might not be returning. My death would leave my wife alone to raise our son, and our expectant daughter, who would be born when I was away. My wife, Anna, was the love of my life, and had been for many years. When we first met at New Albany High School in 1900, she was a junior and I was a freshman. She was the daughter of a local physician whose office was on Spring Street right across from the high School. My infatuation with her would grow through the years, and culminate in my proposal of marriage in 1914. It had taken ten years for our relationship to blossom. I would marry her in 1915 and bring her to Seattle to live our lives. We would live happily near the waters of Puget Sound, in a small house on Alki Beach near the Stockade Hotel. I had lived at the hotel upon my arrival in Seattle 7 years prior. Our son, Will Jr., was born in March, 1916. We were so happy with the opportunities in Seattle, our freedom from social restraint, and the absence of interference from both our families in Indiana and Kentucky, and the start of our new family. It was hot and muggy day in Seattle as I packed my medical bag, uniforms, and personal items for what could be my last trip on earth. As I kissed my wife and son goodbye, I departed our home in West Seattle at Alki Beach for Camp Murray located fifty miles to the South.

Alki Residence 1916

The "Isolation Policy" adopted by the U.S. Congress had been in place since the commencement of hostilities in Europe in 1914. President Wilson supported the policy, being a pacifist, and former college educator. The sinking of the "R.M.S. Lusitania" on May 7, 1915 by a German U-Boat off the coast of Ireland was a stark warning of the German aggression which brought the United States into the war. The British had blockaded the German ports on the Baltic Sea, and thereafter, Germany declared the seas around the United Kingdom as a war zone. The German Embassy in Washington D.C. had placed an advertisement in the newspaper warning the American people of the dangers of sailing on the Lusitania. The deaths of 128 Americans that were on the ship was just cause for the declaration of an act of war. The British had introduced Q-Ships in 1915 with concealed guns. At the time of the sinking, the six inch guns on the ship were unarmed. The Germans justified the sinking and their treating of the vessel as a war ship, because the ship was carrying hundreds of tons of war munitions. There are theories that the British deliberately put the passengers and crew at risk to draw the United States into the war. The sinking of the ship was a factor in the declaration of war which brought me into the military.

My own personal opinion of the war, based on the newspaper reports and news reels at the local theatre, was it was Germany's attempt to bring England and France to surrendering their vast holdings in Africa and Asia, including India, Morocco, and the Middle East. The conflict over foreign lands, and the clash of the Austrian-Hungarian, Ottoman, and European nations was so far from the interests of the United States, I felt there was just cause to stay out of the war. Going into battle to treat the injured and wounded was not my choice. There was no choice given under the new draft act, and it was either go to war or go to jail. The latter wasn't a good alternative given my status in society.

U.S.S. Lusitania Sinking 1915

The unit to which I had been assigned was the Washington Field Hospital located at Camp Murray. The Washington National Guard unit to which I would be assigned following my reporting for duty would be disclosed after my arrival. The U.S. Army was reorganizing, and at that time called upon each state's national guard units for men to serve. There was great uncertainty, and it seemed no one knew what was coming next. The training for which I was assigned to complete was military medical corp. training. The mission of medical services detachment in a combat zone, included training, surgery and treating the wounded, and burying the dead soldiers from the fighting. The military had their own organizational methods, and I would be thoroughly indoctrinated in their military protocols. At age thirty two I felt like a senior officer, but as a first lieutenant, I was at the bottom of the regimental chain of command. Having no seniority, no prior military training, or understanding of military medical rules I was at the mercy of the system. It was under these circumstances I would dedicate my entire being for the next twenty-two months of my life.

∙∙∙

CHAPTER TWO

Reporting for Duty

After reporting for duty at Camp Murray, Washington on August 31st, 2017, I was assigned to the Washington State Field Hospital. As a licensed physician, with practice experience of nine years, I was inducted as a first lieutenant into the medical corp. My experience as a surgeon had been limited. It didn't include treating battle trauma and gunshot wounds. I would be trained in treat every battle injury and wound, including head injuries, amputations, abdominal wounds, and other field injuries. The initial training at the Washington Field Hospital covered the protocols of treatment, from the time of the injury or wound, transport time, triage and ultimately an operation in the surgical theatre. These

Washington State National and Headquarters 1917

steps were to be drilled into each member of the medical corp. assigned to the sanitary train.

The "Sanitary Train", was the term assigned to the medical section of the Company composed of support personnel that attended to the medical needs of the officers and enlisted personnel in an infantry division. A division had one thousand men assigned for duty. The division had four departments, called "trains", namely the ammunition, supply, engineer and sanitary units. The role of the sanitary train was to provide medical care through the establishment of ambulance and field hospitals, and infirmaries in the training, and battle areas. The battle assignments of men and women which would make up the personnel of the medical train, depended on the skills and jobs of each. The transport staff were men trained in picking up wounded or injured soldiers, and transporting them to a field dressing station, a field hospital or a division hospital. The

Horse Drawn Ambulance 1918 France

transport was by horse drawn ambulances or motor ambulances. Each division was divided into ten companies. Each section in the Division was comprised of four companies, and each had 36 motor ambulances, and 12 horse drawn ambulances. The medical personnel transporting the injured and the wounded had to be specially trained not to further injure the casualty, and to safely transport by liter or assisted by foot to the dressing station or field hospital.

A main dressing station would be staffed by one officer and 15 medical personnel, and the station would be located 1,500 to 2,000 yards from the battle field. Due to the danger associated with shelling, rifle fire, grenades, and other munitions, the location of the dressing station had to be relatively safe. During the training we were taught how to arrest hemorrhaging wounds, adjust dressings and bandages, administer morphine and anti-tetanus serum, and treat for shock and gas exposure.

The field stations were broken into four separate departments: receiving and forwarding, dressing, orthopedics and gas. This method of administering patient care could quickly unload, sort and classify new patients. Those capable of being quickly treated were assigned to doctor, so they could return to their unit. The Medical Corp. training we received at the Washington Field Hospital was an adjustment from civilian medical care. Military protocols were more structured than the practices used in civilian clinics or hospitals.

I was active in this training period during the month of September, 1917, and waited orders for my next assignment. On October 5, 1917, my orders came to join the 164th Ambulance Company, and ship out to Camp Greene, North Carolina for basic training. As an officer I would be held to a higher standard during training, and I was anxious to learn the full extent of my training.

• • •

CHAPTER THREE

Camp Greene, North Carolina

Camp Greene, NC 1918

The orders for U.S. Army training came through with an assignment to Camp Greene, North Carolina, outside of Charlotte, North Carolina. Camp Greene was named after the Revolutionary War hero, Nathanael Greene. Nathanael Greene had fought under the command of George Washington, and was a major general of the Continental Army in the American Revolutionary War (1775-1783). He emerged from the war with a reputation as General George Washington's most gifted and dependable officer. He is known for his successful command in the Southern theater of the Revolutionary war.

Camp Greene was established in 1917 for newly enlisted U.S. Army inductees, specifically, to prepare them for combat and service in the First World War. At time, the population of Charlotte was approaching 46,000, and there were an equivalent number of 40,000 soldiers who trained at Camp Greene during the two years that the camp was open.

The United States, at the time of the Declaration of War against Germany in 1917, had a standing army of 250,000 men. The need for additional troops was filled with the National Security and Conscription Act of 1917, and the induction of two and one-half million men. The draft had included all men between the age of eighteen and twenty-six initially. It was amended and expanded to include all men between the age of eighteen and forty-five that were fit for service. The draft notice initiated would be sent to seven million men. It was the first conscription of men from the civilian population since the American Civil War. The government was unprepared for the European War. In order to prepare for war, the U.S. Government authorized the U.S. Army to draft training manuals, appoint and promote military instructors, build rifle ranges, and barracks, order and purchase munitions of all types, and fill leadership positions in a very short period of time.

The train ride for the 164th Ambulance Company from Camp Lewis to North Carolina took 12 days, and commenced on the 6th of October, 1917. Getting to know the men of the 164th Ambulance Company was a new experience for me. All the men were conscripted from civilian life under the National Security and Conscription Act of 1917. We were only in camp at Camp Greene for one day when orders came to combine the 164th Ambulance Company, with the 161st Ambulance Company, which was part of the Second North Dakota Regiment. Combining men from two different states and significantly different regions made the military effort truly national. Men from all walks of life comprised the companies that were merged. For every medical doctor, a support staff of up to fifty was necessary to carry out the duties of the sanitary train. The merger was uneventful, and the two units were combined to create the 164th Ambulance Company. The number of men of the Company was increased to the regulation full strength of an ambulance company of 122 men. The training at Camp Greene was basic with drilling, physical training, weapons practice, and physical examination for fitness.

The weapons training was solely on the use of a 45 caliber hand gun, made by the John M. Browning Arms Company, Model Number M1911. It was a single-action, semi-automatic, magazine-feed pistol which was made specifically for the U.S. Army. As a physician the small arms training at Camp Greene wasn't difficult from a physical standpoint, but mentally I didn't want to shoot anyone. I was also worried about a misfire or accident on the range that could end my life or cause an injury which would end my surgical career. I honestly felt I was drafted as a doctor to treat the injured and wounded. I never imagined killing another human being in the service of my country. Self-defense and personal preservation definitely came into my mind as I was shooting. The rigors of training for war brought challenges that I never thought of. The physical stamina, proper diet, and a good mental attitude towards the mission were critical to the success of our army in the war. The exercise this discipline drummed into each soldier had a price, which was the loss of personal choice.

After several weeks of training at Camp Greene, we were allowed to fraternize with the local North Carolina population in Charlotte. The Southern spirit of hospitality, was extended as the town's people hosted parties at their homes, churches, community halls and parks made us feel welcome. Many lasting life-long friendships were made with the families of Charlotte by the men in our company.

We drilled and participated in a formal military parade as a part of the 2nd Liberty Loan Drive to raise funds for the war effort through the sale of war bonds. The people of Charlotte were generous and supportive in the

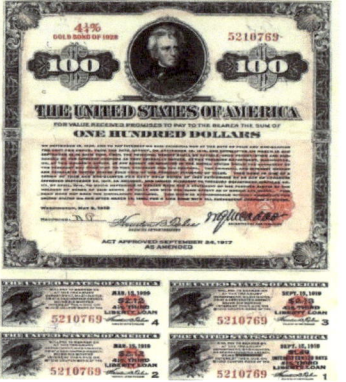
Liberty War Bond 1918

purchase of the war bonds as a part of the drive. The lack of funds in the national treasury called for the issuance of war bonds to support the cause. The government printed posters, held military parades, had song writers write songs to create the patriotic spirit in support of the war. Liberty War Bonds were issued in a variety of denominations. Subscribing to the war bonds became a symbol of patriotic duty in the United States, and introduced the idea of financial securities to many citizens for the first time. The 1st Liberty Loan Act, in April, 1917, established a $5 billion aggregate limit on the amount of government bonds issued at 30 years at 3.5% interest, redeemable after 15 years. It raised $2 billion with 5.5 million people purchasing bonds. The 2nd Liberty Loan Act, in October, 1917, established a $15 billion aggregate limit on the amount of government bonds issued, allowing $3 billion more offered at 25 years at 4% interest, redeemable after 10 years. The amount of the loan totaled $3.8 billion with 9.4 million people purchasing bonds.

We were told of the problems selling the bonds, and the need to support the effort. The response to the first Liberty Bond was unenthusiastic and although the $2 billion issue reportedly sold out, it probably had to be done below par because the notes traded consistently below par on the street. One reaction to this was to attack bond traders as "unpatriotic" if they sold below par. The Board of Governors of the New York Stock Exchange conducted an investigation of brokerage firms who sold war bonds below par to determine if "pro-German influences" were at work. The board forced one such broker to buy the bonds back at par and make a $100,000 donation to the Red Cross. Various explanations were offered for the weakness of the bonds ranging from German sabotage, to the rich not buying the bonds because it would give an appearance of tax dodging (the bonds were exempt from some taxes).

A common consensus was that more needed to be done to sell the bonds to small investors and the common man, rather than large concerns. The poor reception of the first issue resulted in a convertible re-issue five months later at the higher interest rate of 4% and with more favorable tax terms. Even so, when the new issue arrived it also sold below par. This weakness continued with subsequent issues, the 4.25% bond priced as low as 94 cents upon arrival.

The Secretary of the Treasury, William Gibbs McAdoo, reacted to the sales problems by creating an aggressive campaign to popularize the bonds. The government used a division of the Committee on Public Information called the Four Minute Men to help sell Liberty Bonds and Thrift Stamps. Famous artists helped to make posters and movie stars hosted bond rallies. Al Jolson, Elsie Janis, Mary Pickford, Douglas Fairbanks and Charlie Chaplin were among the celebrities that made public appearances promoting the idea that purchasing a liberty bond was "the patriotic thing to do" during the era. Even the Boy Scouts and Girl Scouts sold the bonds, using the slogan "Every Scout to Save a Soldier". Beyond these effective efforts, in 1917 the Aviation Section of the U.S. Army Signal Corps established an elite group of Army pilots assigned to the Liberty Bond campaign. The plan for selling bonds was for the pilots to crisscross the country in their Curtis J4 "Jenny" training aircraft

Liberty Bond Poster 1917

in flights of 3 to 5 aircraft. When they arrived over a town, they would perform acrobatic stunts, and put on mock dog fights for the populace.

After performing their air show, they would land on a road, a golf course, or a pasture nearby. By the time they shut down their engines, most of the townspeople, attracted by their performance, would have gathered. At that point, most people had never seen an airplane, and not ridden in one. Routinely each pilot stood in the rear cockpit of his craft and told the assemblage that every person who purchased a Liberty Bond would be taken for a ride in one of the airplanes. The program was successful in raising a substantial amount of money which was used to pay for the war effort. We were all proud to help the cause of selling the bonds given the need to pay for the war supplies, payroll and munitions.

The medical personnel in the sanitary train were all subject to medical examinations, including inoculations for the prevention of typhoid fever and vaccinations against small-pox. The rigorous medical examinations resulted in the elimination of those physically or medically unfit for overseas service. Those discharged were sent home, released from military service. I passed all physical examinations, was inoculated, and given a passing grade to proceed for all duty.

After a two month period, we received orders to travel to Camp Mills, in Long Neck, New York for training prior to transfer to the European Theatre of War as a part of the American Expeditionary Forces.

• • •

CHAPTER FOUR

Camp Mills, New York

The train travel from North Carolina to New York on a civilian train was with the military transportation mode of the day. Regular passenger trains were filled with troops to capacity, and the travel was non-stop. Meals were field rations or sandwiches with coffee and water served often just twice a day. No one was going to gain weight during field maneuvers or station transfers. As an officer the U.S. Army we were provided upgraded meals and quarters even during transfer from station to station. The three days in route to Camp Mills was filled with conversation, card games, time for reading military manuals, and for rest. Our scenic travels had us traveling through North Carolina, Maryland, Pennsylvania and New Jersey before we arrived at Mineola, New York on October 29th, 1917.

We disembarked the train, and marched in formation to Camp Mills, New York, named after Albert I. Mills, a Major General who was awarded the Medal of Honor in the Spanish American War. The camp, which was located 10 miles from the east of New York City on the Hempstead Plain, on what is now the City of Garden City, New York. The camp was one of three camps operated under the control of the New York Port of Embarkation, for the shipping of troops to Europe for the war. The other camps built were the Aviation General Supply Depot and Concentration Camp, Hazelhurst Field (later Roosevelt Field), and Mitchell Field.

The Camp would be the home to 40,000 transient troops encamped for debarkation to the European Theatre. Wooden barracks would be constructed later during the war for thousands of troops that would travel to fight for the end of the First World War. The camp would eventually consist of 1,200 buildings, which could house 46,000 troops, half in barracks and half in tents. The camp also included a 500 inmate detention camp for prisoners of war, and a permanent garrison run by 5,500 military soldiers. We were the second division to arrive at the newly constructed camp. We found none of the improvements which were later made to the facility. Pitching our tents in the rain we commenced training for our deployment to Europe. The conditions at Camp Mills were similar to what we would find in France. The lack of secure housing was the norm, and as soldiers we were expected to endure difficult conditions. The daily routine of duty during basic training would start at sunrise and end at sunset. We were billeted in tents with kerosene lamps, so we would train during daylight which would save us "from burning the midnight oil". This phrase would come out of this era of U.S.

Camp Mills, New York 1917

Army training, as the U.S. Army refused to issue additional supplies of kerosene oil to the troops. "Getting it Done", was the phrase our Commanders adopted to make us more efficient in our daily assigned tasks. Marching, drilling, training, shooting and keeping our camp in perfect order filled our days. We used to say that all this military training was making us better men. In hindsight, the discipline that we were taught helped save lives when we were in France treating the wounded and injured men. The long hours training was just a warm up to the hours in the field marching, running, doing calisthenics, pitching our tents, maintaining our field gear, and learning to be better soldiers. At the time we thought the Army was pushing us too hard. Getting toughened up was a process that should have taken months. We didn't have months to get tough, so we were pushed extra hard during training. Our Training officer had told us that our service would be the most difficult task in our life. Now in writing this memoir and looking back, I now realize that he was one hundred percent correct.

      The life of a soldier, including officers, wasn't an easy one. Living out in the elements 24/7 was harsh in the winter months. The rain and cold in November 1917 were truly excruciating and living outdoors in a tent would harden any man. Staying warm was the hardest thing we had to do. Having grown up in Indiana on a farm, I was used to hardship and hard work. I was the fourth of six children born on the family homestead that I been built by my grandfather. None of the four boys in our family had stayed on the farm. My older brother, Sam, was a radio engineer, and worked for Westinghouse in Pittsburgh. My older brother, Edwin, was a Captain in the U.S. Navy, as he had attended the Naval Academy at Annapolis, Maryland. My youngest brother, Jim, worked in a factory producing wood panels and veneers. The farm I grew up on in Laconia, Indiana, was a thousand acres, and we grew up growing perishable vegetables, potatoes, soy beans, and hay. All was transported by barge down the Ohio River for sale in big cities along its banks. My youth was spent laboring in the fields, until I was old enough for high school.   I started medical college at nineteen years of age, never to return to the rigors of the agricultural life. Once I left the farm for medical college I never intended to return permanently to the family home at Cedar Farm.

Finding myself at Camp Mills was truly a return to the rural life I had sought to escape. Soldiers were taught to rough it, and move forward without any thought of suffering. The only bright spot in our training was the home visits we were allowed off the camp. The people of New York welcomed our troop with open arms. Given liberty to visit New York City over the Thanksgiving Holiday, we would be welcomed into the homes of many families in the greater New York City area. Given the weather, I was fortunate to meet a host family, and board with them during the weeks prior to our departure to France. The patriotic fever had swept the nation, and the fight for freedom was contagious, and lifted the spirit of all Americans. The Howard Smith family of Long Neck, New York hosted myself and Lt. Diederich Brunjes. They treated us with great hospitality, and the turkey dinner on Thanksgiving was truly one of the best of my life. Snow and below zero cold weather kept the troops from drilling following the Thanksgiving break. It was winter in the Northeast, and everyone was excited to pack up and ship out to France.

The officers I was serving with were Lt. Diederich Brunjes, Lt. Fred L. Horton, Lt. Clifton M. Rosin, and Lt. Gordon L. McClellan. The units came from Washington, Oregon, Montana, Idaho, Wyoming, North and South Dakota, Colorado, New Mexico and Washington, DC. Diederich Brunjes was of Dutch descent and had lived in Colorado. He was raised on a farm, as I had been, and was used to hardship and work. Fred Horton was from Wyoming, and was a cowboy at heart. Gordon McClellan was from Nampa, Idaho, and was raised on a potato farm. He would ultimately take command of the unit, and receive a promotion to Captain. Cliff Rosin was from Wilmington, Delaware, and we were not certain how he had entered the National Guard units which formed the 164th Ambulance Company. The backgrounds of the men I served with were so diverse that it was difficult to form any pattern of how they were selected for service as a part of the military draft. All were dedicated doctors with plenty of experience, and a willingness to serve our country. We all had started out in the 116th Sanitary Train attached to the 161st Ambulance Company, which was part of the 41st Division. We would all be reassigned to different units, and I was assigned and became a part of the 42nd Division, which was known as the "Rainbow Division". I had started out being assigned to

the 41st Division, which was the "Sunset Division". It could be said that I saw rainbows and sunsets during my service in the war. The "Rainbow Division" was formed from state national guard units in twenty-six states.

Rainbow Division Shoulder Patch 1917

When the war started, President Woodrow Wilson was concerned that calling up men for the military from selected states would show favoritism. Then, Major Douglas MacArthur, later a five star general, had the idea of taking men from national guard units across the country to form one unit. By combining men from states all across the county to the call of duty in one unit, the service call would stretch across the country like a rainbow. He was promoted to the rank of colonel following this idea, and made the division's chief of staff. The unit would stand out as one of the most heroic in the war. The division was commanded by General John J. Perishing, the famous military commander that led the campaign against the Mexican bandits in 1912. General George Patton and General Douglas MacArthur, then a captain and a colonel, were both wounded in the war at the same time as members of the unit

I was always worried about getting close to my fellow soldiers, and then then losing them during the battle. The grief of losing a compatriot and friend could interfere with the performance of your medical duties, and bring on depression. I learned not to be too attached to anyone, as there would be no time for personal sadness. In spite of those feelings, I grew close to my fellow medical officers that were called out of civilian life to serve. We had a lot in common after losing our medical practices upon being drafted, and then leaving our wives and children behind.

The assembly of a sanitary train was the primary goal of the 164th Ambulance Company. This included the creation of the administrative body which would support each medical unit. The Company was given twelve ambulances. Some medical units used animal drawn ambulances, which were issued seventy mules and twenty-four horses to pull the ambulances. The men in charge of the animals were like grooms at a stable, caring for the mules and horses. The organization of dressing stations, field hospitals, and regimental hospitals was a major undertaking. The First Division had ten thousand men assigned to its segregated companies. There were at total of 927 officers and men in the First Sanitary Train serving in the Division. The goal was to treat medically all who needed medical services, including the sick, injured, disabled, gassed and mentally afflicted. The supplies necessary to complete the sanitary train's mission were significant. The supplies included all medical supplies, blankets, litters, anti-gas suits, hot water bottles, tourniquets, burial bags, and drugs.

At Camp Mills the company was organized for overseas duty. A new hospital company was formed and transferred to the 164th Infantry Company. Many of the men I served with at Camp Lewis, Washington were among those transferred. Little did I know that I would be transferred to a separate detachment once we were entrenched in the battle field.

On the 11th of December, 2017, our unit packed up and was taken on the Long Island Railroad from Garden City, New Jersey and to Long Island City, New York. The division then boarded a large ferry boat which traveled down the East River to Hoboken, New Jersey. At Pier Fifty Six in Hoboken, we passed off our last letters home at the post office, and boarded the U.S.S. Antigone, our transport ship across the Atlantic Ocean. The letters I sent arrived by U.S. Mail one week after my departure informing my wife, Martha, and son Will that I had left the country for France.

U.S.S. Antigone 1917

● ● ●

CHAPTER FIVE

The Trip Across the Atlantic

On the 12th of December, 1917 we braced ourselves aboard ship for the long trip across the Atlantic Ocean. Our transport, the U.S.S. Antigone, was one of six ships in a convoy to make the voyage across the Atlantic Ocean. The sixteen day trip on the U.S.S. Antigone across the ocean was fraught with danger. The ship was a converted German tramp steamer, that had been confiscated by the U.S. Government at the start of the war. The German crew had attempted to scuttle the vessel by damaging the cylinders on the large engines. The U.S. ship fitters at a shipyard had restored the ship by skillfully welding the cylinders back into working order. The ship was of medium size, and accommodated 2,500 men, in addition to the 600 crew members. We were fed twice a day, and given freedom to travel the well decks on the ship.

After boarding, the ship was towed to a position off Long Island, where it was anchored for two days waiting to join a convoy. The five ships, which would make up our convoy, were the "Susquehanna", "Pres. Lincoln", "The Covington", and Kalb". The convoy was guarded by the battleship cruiser, "North Carolina", until the German U-Boat "danger zone" was reached. In the "danger zone' the convoy was met by a small fleet of destroyers. The "Pres. Lincoln" and the "Covington" would be later sunk by U-Boats upon their return trip from Europe back to the United States.

Convoy of Ships to France 1917

As we departed on the night of December 14th, 1917, we all prayed for our safe return. The task of going to war against the Germans weighted heavily on each one of us. The journey across the Atlantic was nerve wracking, and filled with many anxious moments. There were abandon ship drills routinely, and the crew practiced target practice with the ship's guns. The voyage was mostly uneventful, but on December 27th, 1917 we were attacked by a German U-Boat of the coast of Ireland. Fortunately, the two torpedo fired missed their target. During the battle, one of our destroyers sank the U-Boat. Immediately after the attack land was sighted, and joyously celebrated our luck in not being killed in the attack, and the pending new year. On the night of December 28th, 1917, we anchored in the harbor of St. Nazaire, France, just after dark. We had safely, but not without great trepidation, crossed the Atlantic Ocean.

German U-Boat 1918

We stayed on the ship for almost five days after anchoring. Perhaps the New Year's Eve and New Year's Day celebrations were the underlying reason to remain on the ship, but we were never informed of the reason why we had to stay onboard. We debarked the ship on January, 2nd, 1918, in the afternoon, and marched down the crooked, cobblestone streets of the old French seaport of St. Nazaire to the train depot. We boarded a troop train for a ride of one hundred twenty kilometers into the interior of France. The train followed the Loire River, first to the historic town of Nantes, and second to the site of our first camp, at "La Courtine". Upon our arrival in La Courtine, we pitched our tents in a section of unoccupied land away from the French billets. La Courtine was a French Military Camp, and the site of the organization of our Company.

Troop Debarking Troop Ship 1917

The French military camp of "La Courtine" was cold and uninviting to our troops at first. A few of our men spoke French, so to improve our welcome we mingled and conversed with the French troops. At "La Courtine", the 41st Division, consisting of ten companies would be split up and used as a replacement division. Our division was one of five to make up the First Army Corps, and it was the last to arrive in the war theatre. The commanding general designated the 41st Division to be a replacement division, which meant we would be reassigned.

La Courtine, little did I know, would later in my time in France, would be my home for about a month. I was among the 122 members of the 116th Sanitary Train that had been assigned to the 164th and 161st Ambulance Companies, that had merged. The unit, which was identified as Company "G" of the 164th Ambulance Company, was re-designated as the 164th Field Hospital, and was assigned to duty at La Courtine.

La Courtine, France 1918

During the encampment at La Courtine, I had the occasion of sharing time with my first cousin, Lawson Moore. His mother was my father's sister. He was a Major in the 41st Division Army serving as an aide to General Dickman. He located me through the headquarters of the Fourth Army. We had met only a few times during his visits to Indiana, and twice during my visits to Spokane, Washington, where he resided. Our common ancestral bond was significant. Major Moore had been in France for over ten months, as a member of the Staff School for officers. He had previously attended West Point Military Academy, and graduated with the Class of 1910. He subsequently served in the U.S. Army in the first cavalry at the Presidio, and then on Mexican Border during the skirmishes with Poncho Via and Emilio Zapata. After his initial service from 1910 to 1912, he left the U.S. Army in 1912, to start a career. He subsequently rejoined the U.S. Army when the war broke out. I always considered his distinguished service in the U.S. Army as measure of family pride. My brother, Edwin, was an officer in the U.S. Navy, and he had attended the U.S. Naval Academy. During the hours that we had on his visit to our camp we talked about his experience in the war. He indicated that this war was very different from any that had been previously fought. The sear savagery of the trench warfare, use of poisonous gas, and years of fighting had brought the number of casualties and dead to an all-time high. He told me to prepare myself for seeing the worst of mankind, the most horrible of injuries, and the most gruesome deaths imaginable. His candor was a look into the future for the men in our Company. As we parted I gave him a big hug, not knowing if either of us would survive the war. Being his cousin was a great honor, and I promised him that I would do my best. He said he would try to keep track me in France through his connections at headquarters.

Our duty, while serving at La Courtine, was primarily treating French soldiers that were wounded during the battles. The French Army was short on medical doctors, as many had been killed by German troops when the field hospitals were overrun. We were ordered to carry out all medical services necessary to replace the care lost with the deaths of the French medical staff. The original 164th Ambulance Company was composed of soldiers from the North

La Courtine 1918

Dakota National Guard. Members of the Washington State National Guard had been assigned to join the North Dakota unit. The field officers of the 164th Ambulance Company would change during the early days of our duty in France. Captain McGuire was reassigned to attend Command School at Goundrecourt, and Lieutenant McClellen was promoted to Commander of our unit. The unit's work, while at La Courtine, was generally routine. We provided medical education and training for the other ambulance companies stationed there. The war had been going on in France for almost three and one-half years, so the French troops were war weary, depressed and sullen. I would see many cases of traumatic battle stress caused by days and months of bombardment from enemy artillery. The mental fatigue caused by life in the trenches, living in deep in mud, eating poor rations, and enduring enemy artillery fire was evident. It was a view into our future service in the field stations and hospitals which was frightening.   I was subsequently a witness and surgeon to hundreds of cases of injury during the war.

●●●

CHAPTER SIX

St. Aignan, Montrichard, Noyers and Thesee

Leaving La Courtine on the 24th of January, 1917 by rail to St. Aignan, the trip was torturous for the company. The absence of ground transport left traveling by train as the only means of transportation for the troops. We were stuffed into box cars, originally designed for eight horses, for the two hundred kilometer train ride to St. Aignan. One box car held thirty two men, and the limited space required the men to be lay on top of one another in the box car. The agony brought on by the cramped conditions required us to lay partially on one another in a shingle like fashion. The need for improvisation for the transport of troops was a constant problem for the American Army. The economic strain on France, after three years of war, was evident in the absence of food, limited transportation services, and housing.

St. Aignan, France 1918

The town of St. Aignan was picturesque in the valley of the Cher River. We were billeted in private homes that had been abandoned by the French families. The weather was sunny, and with better quarters, everyone in the company was happier. We conducted our training exercises in an around the town, including the lectures on medical anatomy, physiology, hygiene, first aid training, handling of wounded soldiers, and personal conduct standards in France. We only stayed a week, but it was good one. We moved out, marching to Montrichard, which was a town eighteen kilometers to the east.

The town of Montrichard is about thirty kilometers from Tours, where the water of the River Cher meets the River Loire. This region of France is known as the "Garden of France", given its fertile soil for the growing of agricultural crops. Arriving in Montrichard, in the late afternoon, we were billeted in an old hotel in the middle of town. Being assigned to good quarters made it easier to complete our next assignment of building an infirmary for

Montrichard, France 1918

the sick. The town's hospital had previously been operated by a Covenant of Nuns. The number of sick men, given a near epidemic outbreak of mumps, had overwhelmed the Catholic Sisters. It was now our job to build and run a medical infirmary for the town's people.

We conscripted several buildings adjacent to the hospital, previously operated by the nuns, and built medical wards, and treatment rooms. This type of work was more constructive than the constant drilling and training that we had been doing since our arrival in France. During the five weeks we spent at Montrichard working on the infirmary, we got to fraternize with the French people. They were very friendly, and by using sign language, and the translation books given to us by the Army, we were successful in communicating with them. The French were kind and considerate of our welfare and comfort. Our mail arrived weekly from the states, and kept us motivated to do our best work. We found an old building previously used as a wine storage warehouse, and started remodeling it into an infirmary. The versatility of the men in the Company was remarkable given their skills at carpentry, interior design, installing wall board, painting and plastering, and finally making the necessary electrical upgrades. It was like we were given a vacation to perform contracting work, to relieve us from the rigors of providing medical services. The men showed their enthusiasm for the project, and with the help of some of the French towns people, the clinic was built. It would be in operation for years after the war. Truly, it was an act of humanitarian friendship that came out of the horrors of the war.

On March 8th, 1917 our company moved out to Noyers, which was a small town located about twenty kilometers from St. Aignan. We left sufficient men behind at Montrichard to operate the infirmary that we built. Little did we know that the men left behind would be transferred to an independent organization entitled Camp Infirmary No. 2, and remain there to treat the people in the town. In Noyers, we were ordered to build Field Hospital No. 26. It involved finding a location, and building out operatories, exam rooms, reception and offices for the operation of a fully functional hospital. Given the sanitary trains inventory of medical supplies, operating tables, sterilizing equipment, and medical clothing.

Noyers, France 1918

Our Company was slowly being reassigned, small group by small group, to different units. We lost fifty seven men and four non-commissioned officers to different units, of which I was one the officers reassigned. Forty men, and officers were left to complete the hospital that we worked on for the month of March, and part of April, 1917. I was totally amazed that the transfers and reassignments would fragment our Company. The men had developed friendships and trust amongst their fellow soldiers over the last several months, only to have them broken by the Division Commanders. It was so discouraging to see our unit cut into pieces, that we lost respect for the upper command officers. I wondered how the U.S. Army expected it's men to endure the hardships, injuries, wounds and battle conditions without the bonds of their fellow soldiers. It's a miracle that our unit was able to carry on with its mission day after day. Our complaints fell on deaf ears at the staff officer level. It was the old school army of the nineteenth century that was fighting this war. General Black Jack Perishing was in his final command after over thirty five years in the army. He had risen to the rank of a four star general, as the General of the Army, leading the American Expeditionary Forces (AEF) from the onset of the fighting in France. His bold military tactics were blamed for excessive losses. The mission of the army is often at the cost of the foot soldier whose misery, battle fatigue and anguish are dismissed. West Point graduates are the prime candidates to rise to the rank of general. The military tactics were engrained during each officer's education at West Point. I was not of their mindset, and often wondered if other military leaders could have accomplished the same result with fewer losses.

On April 20th I was reassigned with about forty men to attend Sanitary School at Thesee, and to prepare an active ambulance company for action on the front lines. The Sanitary School was being hosted at a chateau in Thesee which had been occupied prior to the war by a French Count. Taken over by the American Army it was nicknamed the "West Point of France" by the American troops. The protocols at the Sanitary School were strict, with personal inspections daily, morning and evening formations, and lights out promptly at 9 pm. Mornings at the school were dedicated to lectures, and afternoons were saved for drilling, and classes on the proper use of the gas mask. It was if General Perishing had come to Thesee, organized the training, assigned the commanders, and departed knowing his orders would be followed.

Chateau de Thesee

During our initial days at Thesee orders were received from the Division Commander to unite the 161st Ambulance Company and the 164th Ambulance Company into one unit, which would be called the 164th Ambulance Company. The company strength was brought to 122 men for the balance of the war. With the combining of the companies, Lieutenant John B. Kinne became the company commander. Captain Kinne, was a fellow physician from Washington State, and had served under General Perishing in the Philippines in 1898. He had returned to the states after leaving the army, and had gone to medical school. When the war broke out the U.S. Army drafted him back into service. He was a capable leader, and one of the few officers that had seen combat action in their prior service.

Following our completion of the Sanitary School at Thesee we were assigned eight ambulances with drivers for our next assignment at the battle front. On May 9th, 1917 we moved out to the Vosges sector and were attached to the Fifth Division to provide emergency medical services to the French and American troops. It was during this period of the war that I started my surgical rotation as a field surgeon treating the badly wounded and injured solders. The field surgical training we had undertaken in the previous five months in France had now proven critical in our Company's ability to carry out the battle field assignments given to us. We were scared to death, but willing to commit our lives to the orders assigned, and the medical treatments we would be making. It was a very daunting experience as we got closer to the artillery barrages that signaled the front lines. The explosions were non-stop, and could be heard for miles from the front.

•••

CHAPTER SEVEN

The Battle Front in the Vosges Sector

The Field Ambulance Company that formed for training at Thesee, moved out on June 2nd, 1918 to Fraize, to join the French Evacuation Hospital 2/29. We had now been designated as Field Hospital 141 while in the Vosges Sector. As we traveled about the countryside prior to our assignment in the Vosges Sector, we were given time away from the battle zone for rest and relaxation. During the early part of June, a group of us traveled to Menton on the

French Riviera. Traveling by train took two days to reach the French Riviera, for time relaxing on the beach, drinking wine, and sightseeing. The war zone was contained to certain sections in the France, so that life in the areas unaffected by the war was normal.

Menton was a center of recovery for many of the wounded and injured soldiers   Menton was featured in a book written by an English Doctor, James Henry Bennett in 1861, entitled "*Winter and Spring on the Shores of the Mediterranean*", as a place to recuperate from ill health. The place became a destination for wealthy English and Russian aristocrats who built luxurious hotels, villas, and palaces. Many of these hotels and palaces were pressed into service as hospitals during the war.

Menton, French Riviera 1918

One of our duties while on leave was to take a tour of the several of the hospitals located in Mention, and to talk to the hospital administrators on the operation of the hospitals. The number of wounded French soldiers lying in hospital beds recovering were too great to count. Hotels which had been filled with tourists were now medical wards filled with doctors, nurses and orderlies attending to the patients in residence. It seemed we never really got too far away from the sights of misery arising from the war. As we toured we were impressed with the immaculate condition of the wards, the clean sheets, scrubbed floors, and the laundered uniforms of the doctors, nurses and staff. The

French government did their best to properly treat their heroes wounded in the war. The five days of rest on the French Riviera were filled with long walks on the beach, trips to the small towns up and down the coast, and nights in the hotels and nightclubs. The French people were very friendly, and in our conversations with them we felt appreciated for our service. After a week of rest, we caught the train back to Fraise, and rejoined our Company. The last two weeks of June, 1918 our company moved from Fraize to Corcieux and then to Langres. These small towns were damaged from shelling by the Germans, and the people welcomed us as protectors. Our time out of Fraize was of short duration as we were assigned to the main hospital which was located in Fraize. We would be called into service for emergency medical service after a major battle, as the the number of wounded soldiers needing treatment exceeded the available regular medical staff.

Fraize, France 1918

The battle, which ensued in the Vosges Sector of France, was close to the old Alsace Lorraine border. This particular sector was used early in the war by the French and German as a rest area. When America entered the war, this sector was used by the U.S. Army to break in new weaponry, namely cannons and artillery, and the commencement of artillery barrages upon the resting Germans came as quite a shock. The chaos caused by this change in activity would make this sector one of the fiercest battle fronts in the war. The French controlled all troop movements and battle assaults, so when we entered the sector we came under French command. The Germans shelled the town of Fraize, but comparatively little damage was done.   The Germans used airplanes for reconnaissance, and when our troops moved into position at the battle front, they were spotted. The artillery barrage which then resulted caused heavy casualties to our men. Our Company was called into service to evacuate the wounded and dead from Fraize to the rear positions.

French natives lived very close to the battle lines. Often civilian casualties were heavy. During this time as a field surgeon my duties were to work feverishly to save the lives of the wounded. The field hospital was located in Arches, approximately five kilometers east of Fraize.

The medical services given to wounded soldiers in the Anould Sector, which was nearby, were difficult to perform due to the steep terrain, and medical protocols used by the French Army. Being assigned to serve under the command of the French was equivalent to joining the French army. The medical protocols set by the commanding medical officer determined who received immediate care, and who would have to wait and die. There were few roads, however, the ones we used were in fairly good shape despite the steep grades. As the allied trenches were on the eastern side of the slopes, the trenches were under observation by the allies, and were frequently shelled. The frequent shelling and steep terrain required the wounded to be evacuated by hand carried litters, wheeled carriages, or motor cycle carriages. The front was a distances of two or three miles to the field hospital. The medical supplies, carried by the medics and soldiers in pouches and sacks, were called "feed bags," by the soldiers. As the number of battles progressed in the sector there was often a shortage of dressings, splints, and bandages. The number of litters available to carry the wounded would vary depending on the

Medical Corp. in Battle 1918

number of soldiers wounded and carried for treatment. It was difficult to keep the evacuation lanes open where men had fallen wounded. Litter bearers worked constantly in the open, and were often under machine-gun and shell fire. They were often walking targets for the Germans, and they would be killed or wounded to impede the medical care. Every medical organization at the front impressed German prisoners into service as litter bearers. If they refused they were shot on the spot. This wasn't in accord with U.S. Army regulations, but the French regulations mandated this action. It was the only way we could keep more enlisted personnel on the line fighting. In certain cases of emergency the soldiers on the line also carried their wounded comrades to the rear for medical treatment.

First-aid dressings and bandages and, when advisable, splints were applied at the first point of care behind the firing line which offered protection from fire. As long as a supply was available, strychnine or morphine was administered hypodermically, by means of the Greeley unit tubes, whenever these pain medications were available. Antitetanic serum was not administered until the wounded soldier reached a dressing station or a field hospital. It was injected to prevent "Lock Jaw", which was the layman's term for "Tetanus". The bacterial infections in any wound causing "Tetanus", would result in painful muscle contractions in the jaw and neck. The antitetanic serum prevented the condition from developing. From the first point where they were given attention the wounded that were unable to walk were carried by litters to the farthest forward location reached by ambulances. In many cases litters weren't available and soldiers improvised. The most popular improvised litter was blouse or

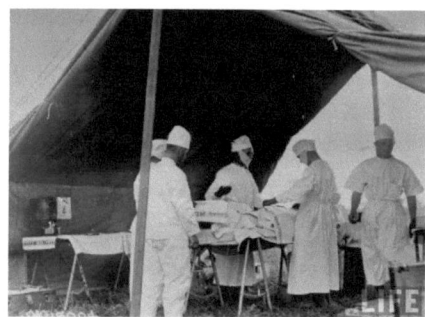
Field Hospital, France 1918

poncho with two rifles used as side bars. The wounded often had to be kept safe and stay protected in shell holes until after nightfall. Any attempt to transport them under fire would often be fatal. The Allied Forces often used

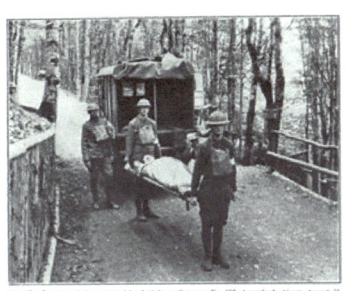
Field Litter Carriers 1918

airplanes for spotting, and purposefully tried to kill the wounded and medical staff in dressing stations or field hospitals by dropping bombs. The ambulances were purposefully parked at a protected post three to five miles from the front, and were called and dispatched by telephone for service. Given this system, the wounded and injured could be quickly and efficiently transported for medical care. There were also field hospitals near to the front that were used to stabilize the seriously wounded until they could be transported to a larger hospital. Regimental hospitals were located at the base of the closest mountain ranges for the seriously sick and slightly wounded soldiers. The largest hospitals were under French command and instruction, and were located in Fraize, Gerardmer, and St. Die.

The field hospital in Fraize was located in an old chateau, and had three operatories, which were outfitted with a stove for sterilizing instruments, cabinets for medical supplies, and proper lighting. There were also rooms for recovery after surgery. The recovery wards were the large eating living room areas in the chateau. The operatories were fitted with a two surgical tables with straps, a head support, and adjoining tables for supplies and surgical equipment. The surgical procedures were usually of short duration given the number of wounded and injured soldiers waiting to be treated.

Hospital in Chateau, Fraize, France 1918

A typical case for treatment would be a shrapnel wound in the leg of a soldier. The biggest challenge in field surgery was the treatment for infection in the wound. Wounds inflicted by shrapnel from an artillery shell were contaminated by bacteria and viruses in the soil. With great preparation the patient would be draped, the area around the wound would be shaved and disinfected with iodine, and the area around would be covered with sterilized towels. The surgeon would put on a sterilized gown, washing his hands, then rinse his hands with alcohol, and have rubber gloves put on up and over the sleeves of the surgical gown.

The patient would be anesthetized with ether poured into an ether mask which was then placed over the patient's mouth. The anesthetist would also be sterilized to effect immediate treatment if the patient choked during the procedure. There were straps on the table to hold the patient in place during the procedure. The area where the wound was located would be painted with iodine, and sterilized towels would be pinched to the patient's skin with pinching scissors. The scalpel, a small surgical instrument with the sharpest of blades, would be used to make the incision. These type of surgeries were usually very bloody as arteries in the hip and thigh areas were cut. The incisions weren't precise, as the cut made were large. The shrapnel that needed to be removed usually laid buried deep in the muscle or soft tissue of the patient. The small and large arteries were tied off after being severed to stop the bleeding during surgery. The surgeon would usually displace the shrapnel with his fingers probing in the soldier's hip, thigh or leg. The metal shrapnel in the wounds varied in size, but generally they were one inch

Surgical Operatory 1918

Artillery Barrage 1918 square, and had very jagged edges. The shrapnel would be covered in dirt, and usually had part of the soldiers breeches clinging to it. The hole made by the surgery would be six inches wide, two to three inches wide, and four inches deep. The wound would be kept open, and Vaseline applied to the edges, while a chlorine smelling disinfectant was used to syringe the wound. The wound would be bandaged, and the patient removed on a stretcher to the recovery ward.

The majority of wounds inflicted on the troops were the result of shell fragments propelled by a charge of high explosive. The large artillery shells were long, tapering, and finished in a cigar shaped casing ranging in size from an inch to a foot in diameter. The largest shells were a foot wide and three or four feet long, and were shot from an artillery cannon having a diameter at the barrel of seventy-five millimeters. The cannon was always referred to as a "75".   The interior of the projectile shell would be filled with TNT or gun powder, which was when ignited by the blasting cap at the base of the shell. At the moment of the shell's explosion the casing would fragmentize into pieces as small as a pin or as big as a chunk weighing a pound. These fragments could be easily stopped by a steel barricade or a soldier's helmet. However, the fragments when fragmented into the body were lethal, give the threat of infection. Infections developed not from the metal fragments, but from the dirt, clothing and bone fragments thrust into the soft tissues. These wounds were called "bottle wounds" given the jagged edges of the wounds similar to the scar made when a glass bottle is shattered and thrust into the skin.

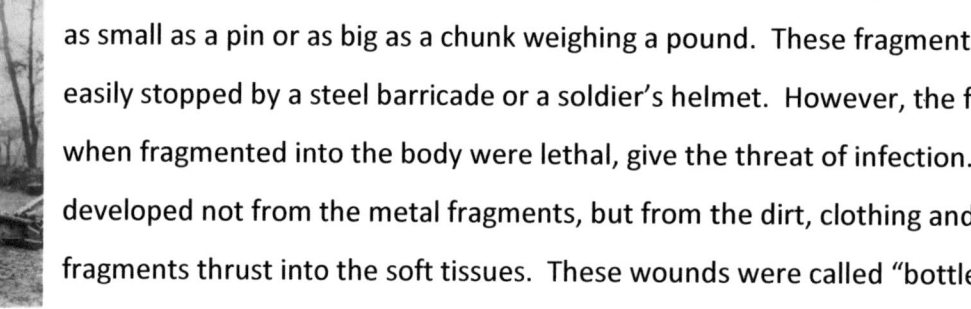
"75" Inch Artillery Cannon 1918

The type of infections that developed in the body which were caused by the contaminated materials varied. One type of infection was tetanus or lockjaw. The antitetanic serum was a blessing for eradicating tetanus. The serum would be given immediately to all wounded men no matter how slight the injury. The "A.T.S." saved thousands of lives during the war. The worse infection arising from shell fragments was thought to be caused by body gases produced during the healing process. This gas infection, called "gas gangrene", was not actually a gas, but it was caused a bacterium known as "bacillus aerogenes capsulatus". Dr. David Welch of Johns Hopkins University had prior to the war isolated the bacillus, and thus it was named "Welch Bacillus" in his honor. The bacillus is an "anaerobic" organism which means that it can only grow and expand in the body where there's an absence of air. The soils in the battle fields of France were contaminated by animal manure, dead animal matter, and other contaminates. Previously used for farming the soils were ripe with this bacillus. The growth of the bacillus in the body resulted in gas bubbles similar to a bubbles produced during the fermentation process in making alcohol. Where ever the gas bubbles collected in the body, they shut off the circulation to the adjoining tissues. Thus, without proper blood supply, the adjoining tissues would die. The gangrene infection would happen so quickly that within twelve to sixteen hours of the onset of the infection, the tissue comprising the body part affected would be totally dead.

The Germans would intentionally bomb field hospitals to push the point of medical treatment further back behind the lines. They did this so more men would die from the bacillus, to extend the time between the onset of the injury and treatment. The more time needed to transport the wounded to a proper hospital for treatment resulted in more soldiers dying. An elaborate system of treatment was ultimately devised by the AEF troops to combat this terrible type of wound.

The easier cases were often mixed in with major injury cases involving the chest, head, back or arms. Amputations to the legs and arms were common. Major surgery was performed quickly and without delay. It was not uncommon during surgery that a chest wound would expose the lungs and heart throbbing bare. There was no time for second thoughts of the seriousness of the wounds as they are presented. Time was always dire, as another case of "life or death" awaited treatment. The medical supplies would flow into the chateau in huge quantities from Paris and Juilly. Ambulances would deliver the patients to the door, and men would carry the wounded on liters to the operatories. Each patient underwent triage, and were subsequently tagged with the preliminary assessment of his injuries and wounds. An administrative assistant would place all personal items belonging the soldier in a cotton-wool bag, marking his name rank and serial number.

Each night the men were ambulanced to Paris to the central hospitals for treatment. The recovery wards in the chateau were emptied nightly so that the hospital was ready to treat the next day's wounded soldiers.

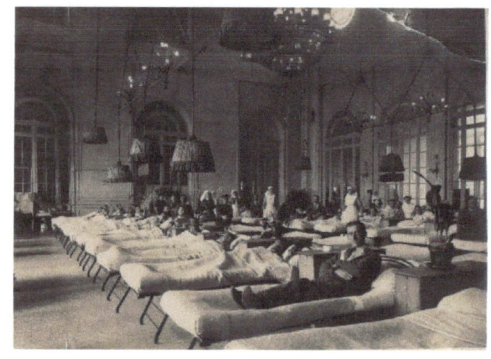

Recovery in Chateau at Fraize 1918

Unfortunately, the soldiers who were mortally wounded, or died during or following surgery were buried in the cemetery next to the chateau. The graves were dug, and the coffins were placed following the last rights ceremony performed by the clergy attending. Phrases of Latin for a Roman burial service were often heard, along with biblical phrases for other Catholic, Protestant, Jew or other religious burials.

It seemed like there was no time for second thoughts regarding the routine which would permeate the medical treatment processes. I often was in a daze after hour of treating the wounded. I had no time to feel empathy for the men I was treating, as it would prevent me from doing my best work. The fatigue eventually caught up with me, and I would have to retire to bed.

The worst cases were the gassing cases where the men had inhaled or been exposed to poisonous gas. The Germans used nerve, mustard, phosgene and chlorine gases in their attacks. There were often times hundreds of men lying on stretchers in an open field next to the chateau fighting for breath, blinded by the gas, or just suffering in a delirious state. Most were crying, moaning or tossing about in significant pain. Dressings were applied to the affected faces of the men, which often gave them some relief. Gas hospitals had been established to treat gassed patients. The gas injuries drove some to take their own lives during recovery.

The work at the field hospital was done on two twelve hour shifts. The work was constant if patients continued to arrive by ambulance. Food was prepared in the hospital kitchen, and served in the dining room at six a.m., as work started timely at eight a.m. When there was lull in the fighting and the ambulances stop bringing the wounded, attention was given by the doctors to those recovering in the wards that hadn't been ambulanced to Paris or Juilly. Cleaning and scrubbing the operatories, polishing the equipment, and writing letters home took up any free time that we had.

The thanks and appreciation that the medical corp. received from the soldiers treated was extraordinary. As physicians, we felt privileged sleeping in dry beds, with clean sheets, and regular food, and doing our jobs. The facilities which the U.S. Army Medical Corp built for the treatment of the injured and wounded were functional and carefully planned. The loss of life in the war was reduced significantly by the sanitary train's protocols administered by the military chain of command. The number of support personnel, nurses, medical aides, and qualified doctors made it all possible. Each hospital was not unlike a civilian hospital in the states.

During the month of July, 1918, the fighting in the Vosges section was among the fiercest of the war following the American Army's commencement of action. The German troops came within forty miles of Paris, and they were thankfully pushed back. The American troops pulled a surprise attack on the Germans and captured Frapelle and Hill

451. Following that battle, the American Army had additional success at the battle of Chateau Theirry. The German Army's ability to recover was lost after these two battles. After four years of war the shear loss of life had reduced the number of fighting men in the French, British and German armies.

We had Bastille Day off, to celebrate the anniversary of the French Revolution, given the fact we were attached as a support unit to the French Army. We returned near the front on July 15th, in the town of Raon l'Etape. This small mountain town was near the biggest battle of 1914, which took place in the town of Ramblervillers. Some 40,000 French Troops perished in the battle fought in the forests of the Ardennes mountains. Graves scattered the mountain road edges for miles, each marked by a white cross. The French people made artificial flowers and hung them on the white crosses. They also made beadwork or used simple garden flowers to adorn the crosses.

Roan l'Etape, France 1918

The horror of the war was evident everywhere, and the common people living in villages had the visual and sensual shock of living it every day. The hospital at Raon l'Etape was named Hôpital Mixte, which was a French term used to identify a multi-use medical facility. During the Frapelle battle, which happened in July 1918, two hundred sixty-one soldiers were gassed. Most were only slightly gassed so their removal for treatment wasn't necessary. There was a special gas hospital at Hôpital St. Charles or at Hôpital Baccarat for special gas treatment. There were always soldiers suffering from gas fright following a gas attack, and many soldiers were identified as malingerers that feigned gas symptoms so as to escape fighting.

The little town of Raon l'Etape was in a valley surrounded by mountains. Once a thriving city, the war had been reduced to ruins. The city, occupied by the Germans in 1914, was destroyed when every building of historical or public significance was blown up. The inhabitants occupied partially destroyed buildings, and hoped for an end to the war. A lot of the roofs of the buildings were still intact, so we used them to be protected from the rain and cold. The temperatures in the summer were good, so the damage to the buildings provided excellent ventilation. Hid away in the woods outside of town was a chateau, called "Chateau Feodal", which was built about 1100 A.D. It was built under the reign of Louis VI, and had a chapel, dungeons, a large court, four large towers with thick walls between, and a large room used for ceremonies. There was a moat of sorts called a "fosse". The chateau was in a partial state of ruin, but as presented it gave us insights into the history of the region.

Chateau Feodal

The town once had several major commercial businesses. There once was a wood and pulp paper mill, a book and general printing plant, a book bindery, and a paper processing plant for the manufacture of writing paper and envelopes. All were destroyed during the war. There once was a large quarry for mining granite out of the mountain adjacent to the town.

Our time in Roan L'Etape was away from the front, and while there it was easy to rest and relax. We grew to know the town's people, and many of us formed friendships that were lasting. The children played in the street in front of our billets, and we would give them candy, sweets and food. Military bands from the French and American forces would play in the evenings in the town square. Melodies from the old South usually sung by minstrels were very popular. The men also sang and danced with the local towns people,

Another tragedy struck at Frapelle after the August 15th, 1918 attack. Men from our Company were sent to relieve the medical corp. on August 21st, that had been serving for six days straight with no rest. A detail of thirty five men from our company arrived at a dressing station just outside of town. They were sitting waiting to be assigned to their designated duty posts when a large artillery shell landed right in their midst, instantly killing three of our men. The bombardment lasted thirty minutes following the initial attack. Our small detachment had been seen by the enemy from a spotting plane from above. The closest German artillery position was ten to twelve kilometers away to the east. With sad hearts we transported our dead comrades to St. Die for burial. The sudden loss of the three men in our small detachment was very heartbreaking.

After the hard work the Commander granted furloughs on September 10th, 1918 for eleven of our company. I was selected, with ten others, to travel to Aix-les-Bains, a summer resort in Savoie, near the Swiss and Italian borders. Relaxing in the sun, eating and drinking, dancing, sleeping and generally recovering from the rigors of the war was our reward for our service. The fatigue caused by long days was catching up with all the troops. Weary from the work, and the sense of loss each of our physical and mental states were wore down. The activity during this time in the war was so frantic and constant, that no one had time to wonder what was coming next.

•••

CHAPTER EIGHT

Life in La Courtine

During the last week of September 1918, my medical group, which was named Field Hospital 141, was assigned back to the military facility at Camp La Courtine, which was operated by the French Army. Having spent two weeks in La Courtine in January 1918, we were acquainted with the camp. The four officers, four non-commissioned officers, and forty men in our detachment were given a support assignment. Our mission was to provide medical service as need at the French military hospital at the camp. After our rest and recovery, the reassignment was a new challenge given the language barrier, French Command, and the fact we would be servicing exclusively

La Courtine, 1918

French soldiers. We had previously been under French Command, so the adjustment to taken orders in French was not new.

The shortage of French medical personnel was the principal reason for the reassignment of our small medical staff. We were transported by ambulances from the Vosges section to La Courtine in about three hours. The one hundred eighty kilometers between the front and La Courtine gave us relief from artillery barrages, and the threat that the Germans would overrun our position. The camp had a capacity of four thousand French troops at the height of the war. At the time of our arrival on September 28th, 1918, there were about two thousand five hundred French military personnel, of which half were providing support, and half were French army troops waiting for reassignment to the front.

Our time at La Courtine was less stressful than being in the field, as we were there in support of the French medical staff. The French doctors always preferred to attend their soldiers. They called upon us to assist when they were over whelmed. As replacements we had more time off than we previously had during any of our time in France.

La Courtine 1918

The battles of July, August and September had taken a toll on the French, British and German armies. They had been at war for four years, and the deaths and casualties drove down the morale of the French troops. The entry of the American Army into the war had also significantly affected the German army's morale. Their chance of victory in the war had become slight with the arrival of two hundred fifty thousand fresh American troops each month. The German army had been overwhelmed by the French and British armies at Amiens early in August 1918, and the news of weakening German resistance had everyone on edge. No one knew at that time what direction the war would take. We worked diligently in the hospital treating soldiers and awaiting news from the front. When the news arrived that that Bulgaria, a German ally in the war, had opened negotiations for peace with the French and the British armies there was great joy. It was definitely Germany's move to continue fighting or make peace. The month of October 1918 was the last major push by the Germans to try to win the war. The number of casualties remained high,, and our support continued.

We were working twelve hour shifts in the hospital, so I started at six a.m., and retired for dinner at six p.m. During my initial stay at La Courtine, in January 1918, I was introduced to the night life in the town of La Courtine, located five kilometers from the camp. The town night life was constant, and the restaurant and bar owners welcomed American soldiers with American dollars. Fatigue compounded by too much night life, and not enough sleep was a big problem. The food served in town was significantly better than the French Army chow, so I tried to get into town at least two or three nights a week for a good meal and a glass of wine.

It was during this time I had realized that I had changed from the zealously serious officer entering the war to an officer performing my duties and awaiting my return to civilian life. I never wanted to advance in the Army, and I remained a First Lieutenant for my entire military career. In order to advance in the U.S. Army you had to show leadership and administrative qualities, and I didn't want to give up using my surgical skills to perform administrative duties. I never wanted to stop treating the wounded and injured, so I avoided all assignments where I had to lead men on selected assignments. My time off the base at La Courtine was the best experience of my time in France.

One could forget for a few hours that the war was raging, men were being wounded or killed, and the line hadn't moved on inch. The futility of the war was maddening, and aimlessly following orders wasn't making a difference in winning the war. Officers, like enlisted men, were subject to court martial for failing to obey orders. It was as if we were mindless souls directed by a higher force.

Town of La Courtine, France 1918

The other officers in our small group joined me as their shift work allowed. The lively entertainment in the bars and restaurants were extraordinarily fun, and the merriment made us all feel that the war was just an illusion. As life was a day to day challenge, the escape to town was always a grand affair. Our favorite hangout was the La Revue de Francaise, a restaurant and bar, that had dancing girls on a stage in the bar. The Moulon Rouge had nothing over the La Revue de Francaise. The Can Can girls dancing and singing French songs would make any soldier forget the war. It was such a relief to relax and forget about the wounded, injured and dead soldiers that had given their all in the fight. Our free time away from duty was permissible if it didn't interfere with the conduct of the sanitary train. Officers were held to a high standard of conduct, so drinking to excess was not permitted. Just being in the restaurant or bar, and hearing the music, and seeing the men dance with the French ladies was very relaxing. The temptation of socializing with the French women was always present, but being married, and an officer made it impossible. The U.S. Army held its officers to the highest level of conduct, and any violation of the officer's code of conduct was punishable by court martial. The number of cases of gonorrhea and syphilis that were treated in the infirmary was another reminder and deterrent to engaging in relations with the local women in the brothels. The temptations were many during the war, but survival was always on my mind.

•••

CHAPTER NINE

Armistice and Travel to Paris

As the month of October 1918 came to an end, word had arrived through unofficial channels that negotiations for the end of the war were ongoing. On November 9th, 1918 General Ludendorff, the Commanding General of the German Army, was relieved of his command. Soon after Ludendorff termination, the Kaiser, Wilhelm II, abdicated his throne, and moved to the Netherlands. Thereafter, a new German Republic was formed by the Social Democratic Party. The new German government sought a fair armistice from the Allied command knowing that they couldn't win the war with more American troops arriving daily. The negotiations for peace, that would commence in January 1919, proved otherwise. On November 11th, 1918 the Armistice was declared, and the war ended. Troops from all countries left the front, and the fighting stopped. With no more casualties the work at the hospital slowly came to an end. The soldiers that were being treated for their injuries were readied for transport to Paris. The remaining French troops at La Courtine were being relocated or sent home. The trains were running twenty-four hours a day, so thousands of men were being transported to other parts of France. The relocation of troops included our small detachment of men who were stationed at La Courtine.

We received orders on November 14th, 1918 to travel to Paris on a new assignment, and not rejoin our Company, which was stationed in the small town of Montigny Le Resle, near Yonne. This was disheartening given our allegiance to the men of the 164th Ambulance Company. Little did I know it was a major blessing as we would be shipped home almost six weeks before the men of our Company.

French Train from La Courtine to Paris 1919

During our service at La Courtine, a major Influenza pandemic had hit all of Europe. Our French Commander gave us an assignment to provide support in the Paris hospitals. The French Medical Corp. reassignment was blessed by the Commanding General of our division. We shipped out to continue our medical service in Paris. The number of wounded French soldiers had overwhelmed the staff at the large hospitals in Paris. In addition, thousands of French citizens were being diagnosed and treated for the "Spanish Flu" or "Swine Flu". The Swine Flu attack became a global pandemic, and medical support from all countries was requested by the French government. As we packed our bags on the 15th of November, 1918, we headed to the train station in La Courtine, and boarded a train to Paris for our new assignment.

The train ride to Paris was six hours on a train that carried only military personnel. Every square inch of the train was occupied by soldiers in uniform either going home, being transferred to a new base, or being reassigned for duty in Paris. The steam engine locomotive was pulling 46 passenger cars and traveling at a maximum speed of forty-five miles an hour. The distance from La Courtine to Paris was two hundred seventy-five miles, over the French countryside, which was spectacular. Through the mountains we traveled North, as we left La Courtine, and proceeded by the towns of Lombarteix, La Fange, Le Mas-d'Artige, Clairavaux and Croze. As we pulled out of the train station just after noon, the entire train erupted with cheers. The excitement on the train was so great, that everyone was wither cheering, laughing or talking. The noise made was so loud that talking was useless as hearing was impossible. The collective joy of the passengers on the train was so great it could fill a balloon with helium which could travel into space. Being in that environment for six hours was exhilarating and exhausting at the same time.

The train's first stop was at the city of Aubusson for water to fill the water tank for the steam engine. The soldiers were allowed to disembark the train for fifteen minutes to stretch their legs, smoke, or get water in the station.

The train's next spot was in Bourges, which was about half way to Paris. Lunch consisted of bread, cheese and water as provided by the French Army.

Bourges, France Train Station 1919

At the stop more water filled the supply tank for the steam engine, and coal was loaded to fire the train's boiler. The line for lunch being served to the enlisted soldiers was a mile long. As an officer, our lunch of bread, cheese, and ham, with jugs of water, was delivered to us by the French Army. Helping the French win the war had its benefits, and being hosted for a lunch celebration was an honor. Back on the journey north everyone simmered down, as we had about four hours to go. It would be nearing dark when the train arrived in Paris and stopped at the Gare de Lyon train station. Finding quarters after dark in Paris carrying our duffel bags and travel cases would be a real challenge.

The last stop before Paris was the City of Orleans, which was famous in France's history back to Roman times. Located on the Loire River the city was historic as the home of the Valois-Orléans family, which included the future king, Louis XII. The travel was constant, so there was no time to see the sights as we took water on, and departed for

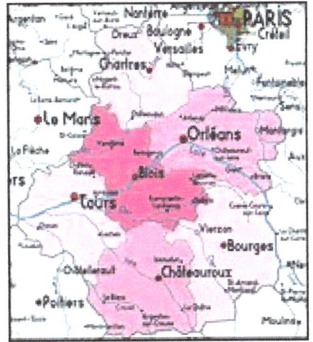
Travel Route from La Courtine To Paris 1919

Paris. We arrived in Paris at 6:00 p.m. which was after dark. The station was a mad house as two thousand troops disembarked the train. Getting our baggage, and struggling out of the terminal had reduced our war weary men to a total level of exhaustion. Everyone moved so slowly, it was like each man had lost all of his body's energy. The crowd was like a slow moving wave that flowed through the narrow exit passages of the Gare De Lyon station and washed out onto the streets of Paris. A military transport sent by the American Hospital in

Paris awaited our small band of men for transport to our new quarters. The military had arranged quarters for us in the basement of the largest hospital in Paris.

Our arrival at the hospital was anti-climactic, as we arrived just after eight o'clock in the evening. We were shown to our basement living quarters by Madame Justine, the head of the house staff. There were twelve rooms, each with four beds and two dressers. The housing was truly a relief after living at La Courtine. The rooms were spotless, with new linens, lighting that was modern, a shower and toilet area which was large. As we retired for the night, we awaited orders on our mission while stationed at the hospital.

As temporary hospital staff we were taking orders from the administrative head of the American Hospital. The original American Hospital was established 1904 for the care for Americans traveling abroad, and was located two blocks from the current site.   The American Hospital had annexed a newly built high school and out fitted the building with six hundred beds, and a staff of four hundred. With the onset of the influenza outbreak each bed was occupied, and the work was constant. We joined the staff to support the care of recovering French and American soldiers and French citizens that had been stricken by the Swine Flu.

The medical services that our small Company added were relatively small considering the hospital employed fifty doctors, one hundred nurses, and two hundred aides and attendants, plus janitorial, maintenance and administrative personnel. The hospital was financed by donations from the American public, and it had been supplemented by the U.S. Government after the start of the war. As military personnel, our transfer was considered a continuing part of the war effort. We worked twelve hour shifts, and filled in where need with every type of medical service. Given our extensive surgical capabilities the doctors in our group had a surgical rotation on soldiers needing additional surgical repairs secondary to the recovery. We had no idea how long we would be at the hospital prior to receiving orders for transport back to the states.

•••

CHAPTER TEN

Duty in Paris

The week after the Armistice, the celebration in Paris continued with all of people dancing in the streets, music and wine, and absolute joy amongst the French people. Any American soldier was embraced by the French as hero, who had fought bravely and defeated the Germans. The affection shown by the French people was amazing, especially the French women who would hug and kiss any American soldier walking on the street. I was taken back by the exuberance of the French, but when I was out in the street and received affection from men or women I perceived it as a sincere gesture, and always appreciated it.

We awoke on November 19th, 1918 and started the day with a full tour of the hospital. There were four floors, not counting the basement, and to insure the location of the different wards, treatment areas, and operatories we needed a thorough knowledge of the building plan. The American Hospital in Paris was originally called the American Ambulance Hospital at Neuilly Lycée, and it was located on Rue Perronet in the Saint-Germain-Des-Prés district adjacent to several universities. The new auxiliary hospital building, to which we were assigned, was originally built in 1911 as a high school, and scheduled to open on October 1, 1914. The onset of the war changed the use of the hospital, and it was turned into an auxiliary military hospital managed by American Hospital organization. The hospital had been operated by volunteer Americans, until April 1917, when America entered the war. When the hospital started treating American soldiers and Americans stricken with Swine Flu Influenza, ("H1N1 Virus"), the U.S. Government provided doctors, nurses, and administrative staff for the hospital. The hospital also took in French citizens when the other hospitals in Paris were full. The wards treating the patients with influenza were sealed off to contain the flu virus.

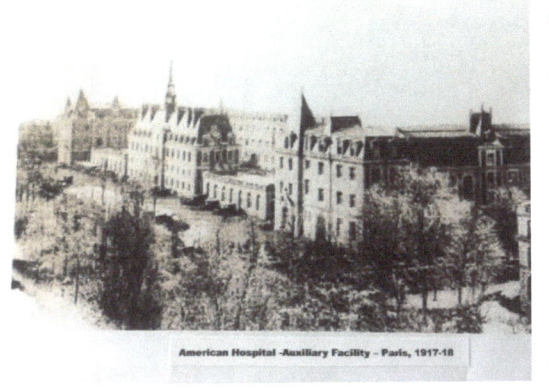

American Ambulance Auxiliary at Neuilly Lycée

We were used to treating war injuries, but treating the sick, stricken by the flu virus was another type of medical service. In order to provide services to the flu patients, each person had to be outfitted with a sterile gown, hat and mask. The pandemic that had initially struck the world in July 1918, and a second surge hit in September 1918. The influenza virus, known as the "Swine Flu" or "Spanish Flu" had become a global medical emergency. A third wave hit in the first part of 1919, causing the deaths of thousands more. Initially traced to an initial outbreak in Fort Riley, Kansas, in early 1917, it could have been spread by U.S. troops traveling overseas to the war theatre. The hospital camp in Roan l'Etape, France had so many cases of influenza, that the U.S. Government believed that the outbreak started there. There was never any official apology issued by the U.S. Army for the outbreak, and no documentation exists which can firmly establish the source of the outbreak of the pandemic. In La Courtine, the number of cases had not been as severe as the number of cases in Paris. The flu caused the deaths of thousands of young healthy people, and the cause was a real mystery. In France, over five hundred thousand people would die by the end of the pandemic in 1920. Treating the patients suffering from the flu was a rigorous job given the constant fevers, night sweats, and pulmonary distresses brought on by the illness. Each patient required constant care by the nurses and medical attendants. Hydration was a major problem, as the most severely ill had difficulty drinking fluids. The demise of many was brought on my severe dehydration, and the onset of pneumonia.

The number of beds for soldiers stricken by influenza increased as soldiers who had stabilized from their wounds were shipped to the United States. Wards in the hospital would open up when soldiers were shipped home, and almost immediately the wards would be filled by soldiers suffering from influenza. As there was no known cure for this strain of influenza, many patients died from complications affecting the body's immune system. The soldiers, so afflicted, may have had complications caused by malnourishment, over crowded conditions in the medical camps,

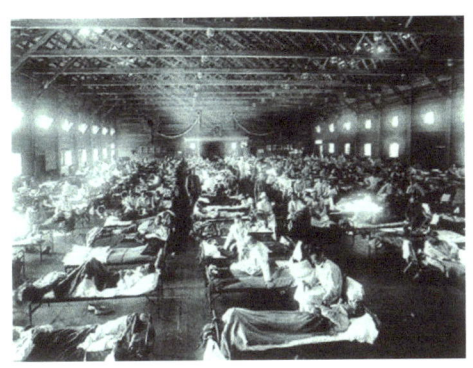

Swine Flu Ward, France 1919

and poor hygiene in the military hospitals initially treating them. Of the cases that we treated at the American Hospital, there was such a high level of cleanliness, sterilized sheets, and available care, most of the patients survived. My service at the hospital was constant, and fortunately, I didn't contract the virus. I owe that good fortune to pure luck, or the intervention of the holy spirit.

The duty of our Company was primarily assisting the badly injured soldiers that were transferred from the war zones. Given the severity of some of the injuries in the last month of the war, we were operating on many cases, where the initial surgery had led to other complications. These included the onset of gangrene, infection, loss of circulation in extremities, blood poisoning, high fevers, and pain management. My duty at the end of my service in France was very rewarding given the high level of medical services I completed at the American Hospital in Paris.

My rest and relaxation time in Paris was significantly greater than my service at La Courtine. I spend time in the cafes, night clubs, and art museums with my fellow officers. The ongoing celebrations in the cafés, bars and clubs in Paris were nightly, and often way beyond my imagination. The pent up energy of the French population after four years of war was released, and men and women openly embraced in public. It wasn't uncommon to see couples in the dark corners of the nightclubs doing more than dancing. It was totally understandable given the strain the war had brought upon the French people, the soldiers fighting, and other displaced foreigners in Paris celebrating. The American soldiers in uniform were expected not to engage in such antics, but Paris was a large city, and I'm sure that some celebrated with the French ladies who were lonely or ones that had lost their husbands in the war.

    The adrenaline of military service that had driven each of us in the in the medical corp. for the last six months slowly started to decline. Our duties at the hospital became were more like a job, than military duty. The twelve hour shifts that had been the norm at La Courtine, were reduced to eight hour shifts, leaving the evenings available for relaxation. I had never spent any time in Europe prior to my arrival in January 1918, so drinking wine in the café's was very relaxing. The French culture was so different from what I knew from living in Indiana and Washington. The nightlife was frantic, and the French always ate dinner late. Dinner at a restaurant in Paris would start serving at 9 pm, and end at midnight. The nightclubs would stay open until 4 a.m., and the bands were playing jazz, ragtime and other new music. Life in Paris was beginning to move in a joyous direction for the first time in many years.

•••

CHAPTER ELEVEN

Paris, Post War and

the Versailles Treaty

Paris Peace Conference, Paris 1919

The Christmas holidays, New Year's Eve and New Year's Day brought time off for our Company with more of the wounded and injured transported on hospital ships back to the states. We still awaited orders related to our transport back to the United States, and the end of our military service. With the war being over for almost two months we were anxious to leave France. That said, the food and wine, had improved significantly with the French resuming their love for drinking wine and eating rich and extravagant foods. We had fresh cheese and bread each morning with ham, foul or chicken. The uncertainty of the completion of post war decisions was resolved with United States, Great Britain, France and Italy uniting together for a Peace Conference. Paris was selected as the venue for the Peace Treaty, and the global meeting would be known as the Versailles Peace Conference. It was held at a variety of places throughout Paris, but the first conference was at Versailles, the palace of French kings, in the town of Versailles.

The history of the Palace of Versailles dates to 1624 when King Louis XIII built a hunting lodge in the forest. Versailles is located twenty kilometers northwest of Paris in the Île-de-France region of France. Louis XIV, the successor to Louis XIII, added on to the hunting lodge, and started construction of the largest chateau in Europe in 1661. It was his design to move the royal court from Paris to Versailles. The King started building around the hunting lodge by adding a large wing, which he named the Plaisirs de l'Île enchantée in 1664. The next expansion was named the *Château Neuf,* and the construction added two new apartments for the king and queen. The apartments which were massive in size were named T*he* G*rand Appartement du Roi, and* T*he* Grand Appartement de la Reine. Significant to the design and construction of the *grands appartements* is that the rooms of both apartments are the same in size and have the same floor plan.   The massive size of the main palace, gardens, and attendant buildings made touring the place more than a one day event. We stayed in a small hotel in the village of Versailles during a long weekend. Our stay at the quaint hotel was so relaxing as we needed to be away

The Palace at Versailles 1714

from the hospital. Louis XIV built the entire place out of his private purse, which made it his personal residence. The opulence of each room was so extravagant that it explains why Marie Antoinette lost her head in the French Revolution. The painted ceilings, walls, doors, French custom-made furniture, crystal chandeliers, woven tapestries, and paintings made it seem like the French King was the richest person in history. The entire palace had a musky smell from years of being shut up. Apparently, windows hinges that opened to let fresh air in hadn't been invented in 1682 when it was built.

The Hall of Mirrors, or *"Galerie des Glaces"* in French, had been the site of many historic signings. The British signed the peace treaty with the United States in 1783 ending the American Revolution. The first meeting of David Lloyd George, Georges Clemenceau, Vittorio Orlando and Woodrow Wilson, the designated leaders of the four nations deciding the fate of the world, took place in the Hall of Mirrors. The Hall of Mirrors was also the site of the last meeting when the nations signed the Peace Treaty which ended the Peace Conference. These four gentlemen would be

, *The Big Four 1919*

referred to as the "Big Four", and the ultimate decisions on the boundary lines of 23 nations, the rebirth of Poland, Lithuania, Estonia, and Latvia, and formation of Yugoslavia and Czechoslovakia. The delegations from over thirty countries were negotiating for rights to vast lands, special legal considerations and reparations from the war. In the midst of this great world peace conference, there were thousands of visitors from every country in the world all wishing for a favorable decision.

The streets of Paris started to be impassable in mid-December 1918, when the world leaders arrived, and starting making political speeches off the balconies of the largest downtown hotels. Ethnic Slavs, Arabs, Japanese,

Chinese, Russian, African, South Americans, Europeans, all gathered as delegates and observers to the Peace Conference in Paris. Our sight-seeing activities came to a halt as moving around in downtown Paris became very difficult during our last two months of service. Our duties at the hospital kept us busy during the day from morning until late afternoon. We were free to take part in the excitement that reigned over Paris, so we ventured to the major hotels where the delegates were staying. We would go to the major hotels, and observe the many different groups talking about their expectations, goals and plans to present to the Counsel of Ten, or the Big Four. It was a very exciting time to witness history in the making.

Hall of Mirrors at Versailles 1919

President Wilson arrived in Paris with a large delegation of Congressmen, cabinet members, advisors, secretaries, and political observers on December 18th, 1918. He traveled by train from Brest to Paris, and boarded an open carriage at the train station for transport to the Hotel Murat, a private residence provided by the French government. We watched, with thousands of people of all nationalities, as he waved to the crowd while traveling down the Camps-Elysees to his hotel. The magnitude of his arrival was so significant as the world awaited the presentation of his League of Nations proposal, which written to insure world peace. We were all hopeful that sanity would return to the world, and future wars could be averted. In hindsight, I was terribly naïve that world politics would change, and the Germans would cease their hostile ways. I had seen the horror of war, and the mass, needless killing of too many good men. To me, I felt the German government should have been neutralized, with all military capabilities and manufacture of armaments taken away. Unfortunately, the Peace Conference in Paris didn't accomplish this task in the six months that it labored on punishing Germany for its heinous acts of war.

President Wilson's Arrival in Paris 1919

I had become very non-political after my induction in the military, as I had seen how the U.S. Military had been used to save France and England from destruction by the Germans. The United States had become an instrument of war for England and France, and most common citizens believed that our government had over stepped it's authority by so acting. The military service forced upon the regular United States citizens by the government was solely to try to gain respect from the French and British governments. It's was true pity that any political gain achieved from the war was short lived. France and Great Britain were unable to prevent the second world war, and Italy joined German and Japan as the evil axis. The Treaty of Versailles, and its harsh treatment of Germany was the primary cause of the second world war. The British Army's failures in the Great War should have been blamed on poor decision making by its generals. It was my view that the general staff of all armies that fought in the Great War were detached from the fighting men who bore the brunt of the conflict. The wounds and infirmities caused by battle permanently altered a soldier's life, thereafter making them limited or cripple.

The freedom of free travel, eating at restaurant, and going to nightclubs and bars that I had enjoyed in my early weeks in Paris also changed with the influx of so many people into Paris. The restaurants, bars, nightclubs and public places were so crowded, the foreigners with money just took over the town. We altered our activities by visiting the Eiffel Tower, the Louvre, the Moulin Rouge, the Tuileries, and other highlights in Paris. It was a city that never slept, and its citizens engaged in a lifestyle that was foreign to me. It seemed to me that France would take many years to recover from the war.

Soldiers were not given the respect they deserved given their sacrifices and service in the Great War. The fighting was over, and now the politicians, business people, and government delegates were more important. I was anxious to leave France and Paris given the change in circumstances brought on by the peace conference. Everyone in the Company was tired of being away from family and loved ones, and each wished to return to their former life.

I often wondered how I would feel treating sick babies, making house calls, working with other doctors in a civilian hospital, being sympathetic to my patients, and running a medical practice. It seemed so mundane compared to the extreme medicine I had practiced in my military service. I also wondered how I would be able to return to my wife and son, and carry with my life as a physician. I knew that many nights would be fraught from nightmares from the war. The first few weeks in January 1919 seemed to drag on as I awaited orders to return to the states. The U.S. Army was transporting five armies totaling three million men back home. The number of ships carrying troops across the Atlantic Ocean totaled one hundred-two. Each ship would take twelve days to cross from France to the United

States. It would take all the ships about three and one-half months to get everyone home. I was anxious to get home in less than one month, rather than three months later.

I heard from my friends in the 164th Ambulance Company. They were stationed in Montigny, a small town about 300 kilometers North of Marseilles. They were anxious to be shipped home as well, but were told it would be sometime after March 19th, 1919. They had been transporting wounded soldiers to larger hospitals, as well as doing repair work to the roads in Montigny. They had been billeted in the homes of the town's people in Montigny, and got to know the families and towns people well. The U.S. Army had purchased cord wood for the town's people to burn in their fireplaces to keep warm. This was of great benefit to the town's people who had very little money. Weekly dances with the French mademoiselles in the town's recreation hall were a big highlight I was told by my former comrades. They told me about the weekly amateur talent shows put on, which featured some of our more talented soldiers. I had told them of my duties at the hospital, and they were impressed with the size of the hospital, and the number of patients being treated there. I told my friends that working in the hospital was like working in a large factory. The injured, wounded and sick soldiers, civilians and others were admitted, treated, restored to health, and discharged while staying at the hospital. Because it was funded by private monies from the United States there was no shortage of anything. My friends were impressed, and they told me it would be good training for a medical position at a big hospital in the states. I hadn't

Montigny, France 1919

really thought about that possibility, but for the last month there I attempted to learn everything about the place, and how it operated.

My hours spent at the hospital had tapered off during the last week of January 1919 with so many of the wounded and injured soldiers being transported to the states. It seemed like such a very hollow place in some of the wards of the hospital that were empty that once had been jammed with patients. Little did I know that after my departure, a third wave of Influenza would sweep through Paris, and the hospital would again be filled with sick people. I was ecstatic when I received orders on January 29th, 1919 to ship out to the states on the U.S.S. Huntington on February 4, 1919 with First Lt.'s Robert Whiteman, John L. Beard, Thomas J. Bland, and 2nd Lt.'s Anderson W. Smith and William L. Epler. My traveling companions for the trip home were from California, Idaho, Maryland and Oklahoma. Regardless of where we all lived in the U.S., returning home and being reunited with our families was the only thing on our minds.

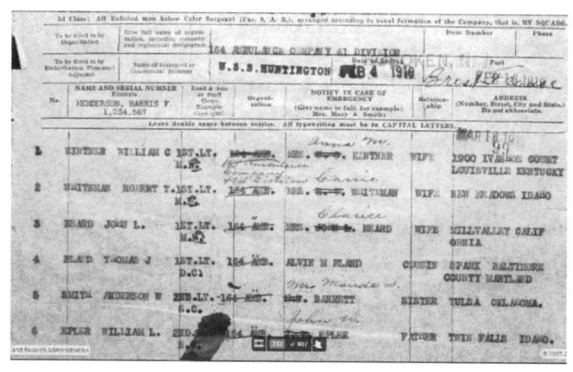
Travel Orders to Return to USA 1919

We received directions from our Commanding Officer to proceed to Brest, France, and the embarkation camp for processing out of the European Theatre of War. The day was overcast, with a possible chance of rain. We could have cared less about the weather on that day, but we had to face crossing the Atlantic once again. The voyage would be much easier without the threat of U-Boats sinking our ship.

• • •

CHAPTER TWELVE

Going Home

The days before February 4th, 1919 were hectic with the completion of paperwork at the hospital, final rounds, packing up, and not getting too excited about departing. The routine at the hospital in the last week had become tiresome work. It was the same wards, the same patients laboring to recover from their injuries and wounds, and the same nurses asking the same questions. Those with severe war injuries would never totally recover. It was the job of the medical staff to connect with each patient, and give them hope. After months of suffering patients often gave up on the healing process and lapsed into depression. There were many manic depressed soldiers who couldn't return to their families until their physical condition permitted travel. There was no treatment for these poor souls who had lost everything in the war. The newspapers has named these returning soldiers, "The Lost Generation", because they had lost so much of themselves in the horrors of war. Time just slowly dragged for those who were so afflicted. I was anxious to get on with my life, and I look forward to my future practicing medicine in Seattle.

The dates in the year 1919 were significant because of the coincidental joinder of the Julian and Gregorian calendars. It was the 1,919th year of the Common Era (CE) and Anno Domini (AD) calendars. When something happens in the time recording process that is totally unexpected, everyone takes notice, and denotes that it's a very special year. The month of January 1919 had been the first month of a new year without a global war in five years. Civil unrest, riots, protests and police actions filled the news in many of the areas where the war had turned neighbor against neighbor. Even in my home town of Seattle, a general strike had paralyzed the city for ten days in January. The Eighteenth Amendment to the U.S. Constitution had been ratified in the U.S. Congress prohibiting the legal manufacture or sale of alcoholic beverages. It was a new era in America as the "Doughboys" returned to the states. However, there would be no champagne parties to celebrate upon the homecoming of America's soldiers.

Waking up on Saturday morning, February 1st, 1919, at six in the morning, was electric. It was our travel day to the coast, from Paris to Brest, and the beginning of the debarkation process for transport to the United States. At the train depot hundreds of Parisiennes came to cheer us off. The train ride was just two hours from Paris to Brest, but the excitement on the train, filled with soldiers that were going home, was beyond any I had previously witnessed. The men were cheering, laughing and telling stories the entire trip. The spirit of victory had raised them to a new level of joy. Being on the winning side in the worst conflict in history made each one of a hero. Everyone was in uniform, and proud to be so. As we approached Brest, and the Atlantic Ocean came into view the hearts of each soldier soared. Just two thousand miles of ocean between Brest and Hoboken, New Jersey separated the men from home. The twelve-day journey would be long, potentially with rough seas, poor food, and cramped conditions, but their spirits wouldn't be dampened.

Gare de Lyon Station, Paris 1919

The train depot at Brest was about two miles to the south of the embarkation station, named, "Camp Pontankezen", which was the depot established by the American Expeditionary Force in 1917. The original garrison at Brest was built by Napoleon Bonaparte in 1804 and consisted of six stone buildings located on fifteen acres of land. There was a seventh building which Napoleon used as a morgue, which through history was named "Napoleon's Morgue". The site selected as the debarkation station for the American troops arriving in July 1917, was the only property which could function for the selected purpose. The original camp had an inside area, within the walls of the original garrison, and an outside area. The outside area was ninety acres at the

Camp Pontankezen 1919

time it was established, but when we it was over one thousand acres. Tents were pitched as far as the eye could see over the hilly terrain, sheltering over one hundred thousand soldiers. The U.S. Army had constructed new steel barracks in 1918, but the new buildings only housed five thousand troops. The site had been built on a very hilly area, without adequate drainage, and therefore the camp was very muddy. Given the mud the U.S. Army made a major improvement by building "duck boards" of lumber which were used as sidewalks. Miles and miles of "duck boards" covering on and over the mud, went to all parts of the camp, The camp site was still primitive with no permanent sewers, running water, drainage system, or a permanent building for food service. Our arrival, on Saturday, February 1st, 1919, went unnoticed given the mass of humanity that was awaiting transport.

The processing of the soldiers at embarkation system was necessary to ensure that each soldier was accounted for. The U.S. Army was slow in processing the men, and thousands had to wait their turn to be processed and assigned to a ship. Our Company needed the nearly three days to process out even though we had orders and a travel date. The U.S. Army had shipped out forty- thousand men in December 1918, sixty-five thousand in January 1919, and were increasing their numbers daily when we arrived. We all accepted our fate of waiting for our turn starting with a routine physical, then filling out and signing paperwork processing out of the war theatre, and then undergoing a psychiatric exam to insure that we weren't suffering from "Shell Shock". When we passed the exam we delivered of our rifles and munitions. During the time were being processed we were released from performing any medical duties, and were treated as any other soldier.

Our assigned tents in Camp Pontankezen were about one mile from the old garrison in a section of the camp known as the "North Forty". The Duck Boards were like sidewalks in a city, and the camp had sections marked by signs. The "North Forty" had ten different section, and we were in Section 46 over half way to the next area. The Duck Boards carried us all the way to our tents, which fortunately all had wooden floors. About half the tents in the camp had foundations constructed with wooden floors and sides to the tent. The tents weren't heated, so the nights were cold, as the wind blew off the ocean, so any protection was appreciated. Camp Pontankezen was built on a peninsula outside of Brest, and surrounded on three sides by the Atlantic Ocean.

Camp Pontenkazen 1919

The two days that we were sheltered at the camp passed without incident as we had acceptable weather. The temperatures were forty-five degrees at night, and fifty to sixty degrees during the day. Given the fact that it was the month of February we felt extremely lucky that snow wasn't falling. Some soldiers in December and January had endured snow, and freezing temperatures. I believed the final days of my service in the U.S. Army were a test of my endurance and sanity. We passed the time playing cards, reading or writing letters home. Informing my wife and young son that I would be home shortly was high on my list of things to do. The mail would go out on the next ship crossing, and would give my family notice of my arrival in the states. Any notice was better than no notice at all after being away for almost a year and three quarters.

I talked with the other medical officers that I was sharing quarters with about their future plans. As doctors, they planned to set up their practices in their home towns. Bob Whiteman was from New Meadows, Idaho, which was a small town near the eastern border of Oregon. The town started as a depot stop for the Pacific and Idaho Northern Railroad and had grown from many that got off the train and stayed. The depot was built in 1910, so in the nine years hence the town was still growing. Bob was joining the other doctor in town to start his general practice. John Beard, my other tent mate, was from Mill Valley, California, located fourteen miles north of San Francisco in Marin County. Mill Valley was a very prosperous community in a rural setting, that grew from tourism by San Francisco's wealthy citizens. The valley had historically been used for farming and ranching. The rolling hills adjacent to the town were not accessible until the North Pacific Coast Railroad extended tracks in 1889. The small town had doubled in size after the San Francisco Earthquake in 1906, and John's return home was going to be prosperous. Opening a new medical practice in a town that was booming offered him a bright future.

I was concerned about re-opening my medical practice in Seattle, with the news of a general strike which paralyzed the business community. I knew a lot of people in downtown Seattle who that had previously been my patients. Perhaps my service in the war would be looked upon as patriotic, and I would be rewarded with people joining my medical practice. We all had challenges to look forward to in our return to civilian life. Whatever those challenges were they were nothing compared to what we had endured in the war.

U.S.S. Huntington

The time passed quickly, and February 4th, 1919 brought our time to assemble for embarkation, and for boarding the U.S.S. Huntington for transport across the Atlantic Ocean. It was in the early morning hours of February 4th, 1919 when we boarded the ship with one thousand nine hundred other soldiers that were going home with us. The "U.S.S. *Huntington*" (ARC-5), originally was the "USS *West Virginia*", and it was the first ship named for the

State of West Virginia. The ship was an armored cruiser, one of three Pennsylvania-class ships authorized by Congress in 1899. The ship's dimension were 504 feet long, 70 feet wide, and the ship had five decks below. On November 11, 1916, the cruiser was renamed the "*U.S.S. Huntington* to allow transfer of the original name to a newly authorized and recently built battleship. Our ship had been converted to a troop carrier in January 1917, but the ship had not been put into service transporting troops from France to the states until one month prior to our boarding.

The officers had quarters separate from the enlisted personnel, so aboard ship we ate in a different galley, and slept two men to a small room. The troops were in hammocks below decks. The trip across the Atlantic was rough, with routinely fifteen to twenty-foot seas, which caused a lot of pitching and rolling, and sea sickness. I had acquired some sea sickness pills from the dispensary at Camp Pontankezen, so I was ready for the ocean crossing. Time was spent mostly sleeping, reading, playing cards, or talking with my fellow officers. It was interesting to talk to many of the field officers that had served in the trenches in the battles at Cantigny, Chateau-Thierry, Belleau Wood, and Cambrai. The uncertainty of life on the front lines for the men that served was unnerving. One moment, a fellow soldier would be there, and the next he was gone, hit by an artillery shell. The trenches were up to twelve feet deep, with entire rooms carved out of the earth for soldiers to rest prior to engaging with the enemy. The battles took a heavy toll on the officers that I spoke to on the ship returning to the states. I felt better about my service in saving lives, rather than sending some poor soul sent out into no man's land to be dispatched to the after-life.

I had not thought about the millions that died in the war. It was if an evil spirit had come to earth, and taken control of the armies of so many countries. It had been a world war, and one that would take decades to recover from. The battle fields of France, Greece, Serbia, Turkey, Austria, Hungary, and so many other countries had been laid waste from the millions of artillery shells fired. The cultural differences and hatred that been the underlying cause of the war hadn't changed. There was still unrest, senseless killing, and small military battles going on after the armistice between the major armies. It was if the population of the world had been reduced in the name of the God of War, Mars.

I was thankful that I had survived the war for the benefit of my family, and for the opportunity to live out my life saving lives, healing the sick, and contributing to humanity. In writing this memoir in the last years of my life, I have relived a time in my life which was filled with death, suffering and misery. Being a doctor prior to the war I had seen these things, but not to the scale caused by this war. I had not been a religious man prior to the war. I began to wonder whether God or Satan was in control of the earth during the last five years. With the end of the war, peace reigned over the earth. As the ship pitched and rolled over the ocean seas I felt a sense of relief that my military service was soon to end. "For God and Country" had been the motto carrying the American troops forward, and now I believed that neither was served.

As we entered New York harbor headed to dock at Hoboken, New Jersey, where my trip to France had started, we passed the Statute of Liberty, given to us by France in 1886. I felt we had repaid our debt to France for the gift of lady liberty with our contribution to the victory in the war.

Docking at the pier, disembarking, and starting the demobilization process, was like waking up from a bad dream. As I left Camp Mills, I was indeed a free man again. The trip across the country by train to my home in Seattle, Washington was delayed by a detour to Indiana and Kentucky to pick up my wife and son, see my new daughter. As a civilian I was no longer under orders, and therefore I was finally free to travel where ever I pleased. I headed to Louisville, Kentucky by train to be with my family, and my wife's family. We were allowed to keep our pistol, uniforms and other small items issued to us by the army. These items would be reminders of my time in France. This memoir is dedicated to those American soldiers who gave their lives for the cause of freedom. The world had been saved by the joint efforts of all the Allied nations, and the late joinder of the American Expeditionary Force.

The years have passed as I write this memoir, but the memories of my time in France during the war haven't. If the horrors of war could have been forgotten the lives of so many would have been better. I honor all those men that served with the memory of America's military effort in the war. God Bless America.

Statue of Liberty 1919

•••

CHAPTER THIRTEEN

The Beginning of the End

The weather in the Pacific Northwest on October 10th, 1949 is mild, as I contemplate the last days of my life. As a physician I recognize the physical signs that my time on earth is running out. My shortness of breath, occasional chest pains, and general fatigue prevent me from regular activities. Facing my declining health, I now realize that I've made some major mistakes in my life. I was foolish to ask my wife for a divorce in 1932 with four children at home. I'm not sure why I had marital affairs, and acted so foolishly at the age of forty seven. I now realize that life is short, and there was no excuse for hurting my wife and children the way I did. The fact that we didn't speak to each other after that day until her death in 1944, made our home a very unhappy one.

I have thought over and over about the stresses from the war. Perhaps seeing the horrors of war brought on a mid-life crisis. It hurts a great deal to have been personally estranged from my children since that day. My oldest son

Will, Jr., has never forgiven me for hurting his mother so. I have tried to make it up to him by selling him the family home and my medical practice, when he returned from World War II just four years ago. My daughter, Nancy Jane, and sons, Walter and Robert, went on with their lives and were successful in spite of my failure as a father. I now realize that my skills as a father were probably absent given the fact that my father was not a good father. I am proud of the fact that I have supported my children in their educational pursuits, careers and family life. I am extremely proud of my children, as two are in medicine, one in dentistry, and one in education.

I often think about the soldiers in the 164th Ambulance Company that didn't return from the war. I was lucky so many times in not being in harm's way, or at a field hospital that was shelled or overrun by the Germans. I had heard stores from my French comrades at La Courtine that told of doctors and nurses that were treating soldiers at a field hospital that was over-run by the enemy. All were shot dead in their tracks as the Germans took no prisoners during battle. The war taught me that life was fleeting, especially if you were in the wrong place at the wrong time. I could have been killed by an artillery shell, like the men in our Company that were killed at Roan l'Etape, or a gas attack that drifted in my direction because of a westerly wind. On my two trips across the Atlantic Ocean the ship I was on barely escaped being sunk by German U-Boats. I often wonder why I was spared, and others weren't. As I write this memoir, those thought flood my brain, and I thank the Lord that I was spared. I feel I have contributed to the world in so many ways. As a doctor and surgeon I saved thousands of lives in the operating room, and inoculated thousands more preventing disease. I served proudly in our nation's army , and raised three sons that served in the military during World War II. Life is filled with the good and the bad, and I have seen more suffering, death and misery than most. I truly hope that his memoir provides some solace to my family members, and their descendants, as an apology for my actions.

As a newly-wed with a new son, and a daughter on the way, my wife and I were truly happy until the United States declared war on Germany. The story of my military career is the subject of this memoir. May the Good Lord forgive my sins, as there have been many.

•••

EPILOGUE

The story, "La Courtine: A Surgeon's Memoir" is told in the first person to add to its authenticity. First Lt. William C. Kintner, Sr. tells his story through the narrative of his grandson, James P. Kintner, one hundred years after the events depicted. The story starts with the receipt by Dr. Kintner of his draft notice to report for duty with the Washington National Guard. The memoir ends the day of his discharge from the U.S. Army twenty-two months later. The story, as written, is presented to the readers as a memoir written in the last year of his life in 1949. His final thoughts reveal his disappointment that the American Expeditionary Forces couldn't end Germany's ability to engage in war. Had the United States, France and England, marched into Germany and vanquished the German army perhaps World War II would not have occurred. This memoir recounts First Lt. Kintner's induction, training, and service in France in a variety of units, as the 164th Ambulance Company was designated a replacement unit. Many of the members of the Company were transferred to other units with no prior notice, and their reassignment fractured friendships and bonds that made their service more difficult. Given the great length of time between the occurrence of the events portrayed in the book as his memoir, there may be some errors or omissions. Please excuse any errors or omissions regarding factual recitations in the book. The absence of military records made the re-creation of First Lt. Kintner's story significantly more difficult. No words can match the personal commitment, valor, dedication and effort expended by the soldiers who fought in the "Great War". The physical, emotional and mental damage, injury and loss sustained by all who served is not dwelt upon in order to focus on the heroic service of those mentioned in this memoir. Focusing on the positive actions of the men of the 164th Ambulance Company was the purpose and scope of this memoir. We should all be very proud of the service of our forefathers in the armed forces of the United States. Without their service perhaps we would not enjoy the freedoms that we take for granted today. God Bless America.

James P. Kintner

Indio, CA
September, 2018

• • •